BEYOND THE MOUNTAINS

BEYOND THE MOUNTAINS

*An Immigrant's Inspiring
Journey of Healing and Learning to
Dance with the Universe*

DEJA VU PREM

COUNTERPOINT | CALIFORNIA

Beyond the Mountains

This is a work of nonfiction. However, some names and identifying details of individuals have been changed to protect their privacy, correspondence has been shortened for clarity, and dialogue has been reconstructed to the best of the author's recollection.

First Counterpoint edition: 2024

Library of Congress Cataloging-in-Publication Data
Names: Prem, Deja Vu, author.
Title: Beyond the mountains : an immigrant's inspiring journey of healing and learning to dance with the universe / Deja Vu Prem.
Other titles: Immigrant's inspiring journey of healing and learning to dance with the universe
Description: First Counterpoint edition. | California : Counterpoint, 2024.
Identifiers: LCCN 2024028899 | ISBN 9781640096455 (hardcover) | ISBN 9781640096462 (ebook)
Subjects: LCSH: Prem, Deja Vu. | Filipino American women—California—Los Angeles—Biography. | Filipino Americans—California—Los Angeles—Biography. | Lesbians—California—Los Angeles—Biography. | Motion picture producers and directors—California—Los Angeles—Biography. | Los Angeles (Calif.)—Biography. | Mail order brides—California—San Francisco—Biography. | Mail order brides—Abuse of—California—San Francisco. | San Francisco (Calif—Biography. | Dipolog City (Philippines)—Biography.
Classification: LCC F869.L853 P74 2024 | DDC 973/.0499210092 [B]—dc23/eng/20240808
LC record available at https://lccn.loc.gov/2024028899

Jacket design by Farjana Yasmin
Jacket illustration © iStock / oxign
Watercolor mountains © Adobe Stock / Olga

COUNTERPOINT
Los Angeles and San Francisco, CA
www.counterpointpress.com

Printed in the United States of America

1 3 5 7 9 10 8 6 4 2

*To Elizabeth Koch, who catapulted this book to life and
inspired me to the deepest dive into the unknown dimension of who
I am. An experience I've longed to embody from the depths of my soul.
This memoir breathes the essence of that awakening.*

BEYOND THE MOUNTAINS

1.

Fly, Baby, Fly

GREW UP IN A REMOTE BARRIO IN THE PHILIPPINES, at the basin of a mountain. My village was surrounded by rice paddies, and I often sat in the middle of them to wriggle my feet in the mud and observe the various stages of the crop. Green indicates the rice is close to harvest. When the crop turns yellow and the crows begin to circle, the rice is at its peak. Beyond the rice were coconut groves, and I'd gaze at the giant vibrant trees dancing against the jagged ridges of the mountains in the distance and daydream about one day traveling beyond this place. Marvels awaited me on the other side. The mountains possessed a weird energy, like another dimension existed behind them. Depending on where I sat, the ridgetop became a silhouette of a person leisurely stretched out with one leg down; sometimes, it was a face with a remarkably discernible nose. My imagination was endless. Though we lived far off the main road,

I could hear the moving cars behind us, and I'd often envision a parallel world beyond the lush landscape—perhaps it was deliberately concealing paradise or something outside the vastness of my creative mind.

My paternal grandfather was a shaman. He passed before I was born. Although we never met, I felt a strong connection with him, even if the thought of him scared me because of the things said about him. I heard Grandfather could do multidimensional travel, that he had access to a gateway to a higher level of consciousness. I only ever heard bits and pieces. My mother was a devout Catholic and raised us in the faith. Mama didn't like to talk about Grandfather's abilities. She shoved it in the dark, believing what my grandfather could see and do was evil, so I, too, exhausted myself trying to push that connection away. But no matter what, I still felt something. I never spoke of what I felt, thought, or saw to anyone, but I believed there was something better or more to life than what I was experiencing. Then, as if Grandfather planted that seed himself, it became a vision that grew inside me. Thoughts of the other side of those mountain ridges were my escape from the haunting reality of the world I lived in.

I first heard of this place called America from Papa when he worked for a logging company in Marawi City. Americans ran the company and from what Papa told me, that place called America sounded far away. One of the general managers, Mr. McCaloney, and his wife lived in a massive home with a guesthouse nestled in the hills. Their house had a breathtaking view overlooking Lake Lanao, the biggest natural lake in the Philippines.

The home had high ceilings, massive rock walls, expansive living space, and a racquetball court at the end of the hallway. Everything in that place was good. Nothing bad. Everybody was happy. My aunt Edith was their maid and cook. Occasionally, she brought my sister and me along. We'd sit on their front porch while Mrs. McCaloney filled our little bellies with freshly baked cookies. I don't remember anything Mrs. McCaloney said because I didn't speak a word of English at the time, but I remember that she played games with us in the most engaging manner.

Outside of their compound, the town was predominately Muslim, and there was a great deal of unrest during the period Papa worked for them. In an effort to take over the company, the Muslims raided the house and kidnapped the Americans for ransom. My entire family evacuated the town because they were barricading the roads, creating widespread fear. My parents grabbed everything they could, loaded it into a big truck, and moved us to Iligan City outside of Marawi until Papa built our home in Sinuyak, where he grew up.

The encounters with the Americans gave me the perspective that America was a safe haven and its people were kind. For some reason, I had the notion that America was somewhere behind those mountains, and that's where I wanted to go—the farthest I could from this suffocating place devoid of heart and soul food, toward nourishment called home. When I glanced around, I thought, This *cannot be all there is to life.*

It was apparent we didn't have much; I was always barefoot or in worn flip-flops with the balls of my feet scraping the ground because of the holes in them. We were married to our flip-flops and clothing until they dissolved. Our streets were made of dirt or gravel, and we didn't have a car. No one in the village had a car, so we walked practically everywhere in the heat and humidity. But there were colorful jeepneys, like little buses, to get around in if we had to go into the nearest city. It wasn't a convenient life, but it was all we knew.

Our house was small and humble, but Mama kept it clean.

To keep the dust and dirt out, she constantly swept with a silhig made from the hard veins of the coconut palm. We didn't have anything other than the basics—a roof, four walls, bamboo slats for the floor with space for an altar and Mama to cook. Mama was a great cook. Rice was a staple for us. In addition, Papa had a garden full of cucumbers, squash, okra, eggplant, and other vegetables that Mama could make incredibly palatable. One of my favorite dishes was Mama's eggplant. She'd pick it fresh, grill it until the skin peeled off, then gently squash it until flattened while intact. Then Mama soaked the eggplant in slightly beaten eggs and lightly fried it to a golden brown. I could taste the love Mama put into cooking in everything she made.

There wasn't electricity, so we used kerosene lamps when we had to. Our bodies were synchronized to their internal clocks. We went to bed before dark and woke to the sound of chickens and roosters crowing. Our house had two beds made of plywood with palm leaves woven into a mat and laid on top for padding. I shared one bed with my older sister and two brothers while Mama and Papa slept in their bed a few feet away behind a partition. We draped nets over the beds and tucked under the palm leaves to keep the mosquitoes away. We didn't have plumbing. We had an outhouse, and I did everything I could to make sure I didn't use it once it got dark. I trained myself not to go to the bathroom in the middle of the night to avoid running into the huge American bullfrogs that lived in there and would look straight at me as I squatted.

Early each morning, my siblings and I went to fetch water from the well in the village, where everyone seemed to gather simultaneously. It took us three trips, walking a quarter of a mile each way. We'd dump the water we collected into our clay tank until it was full, placing some extra containers on the floor next to it so we could refill it when it emptied. Our village's river served as a communal bathtub and laundry. We'd bathe in it fully clothed. Get in, pour cool water down the inside of our clothing with a pail, and get out. Our clothing was thin due to the tropical climate. Laundry was carried to that same river on our heads, washed by hand, and lugged back home to hang dry. Although we all washed clothes, Mama washed them in a particular way—when I put my clothes on, I felt like a different person. I think her love went into the way she did things because other than that, I didn't feel it the way I believed I needed. The same way I wanted to go to America, I wanted to find this thing called *love*.

My family wasn't affectionate. Everyone seemed so focused on trying to survive that there was a looming feeling of irreconcilable distance between all of us. Nobody asked: How was your day? What did you do? Nothing. One time, I climbed a guava tree and got covered with large beige gnarly ants. Panicked, I jumped out of the tree, fell, and got hurt, but I never told anyone because I knew they wouldn't ask the simplest question: are you okay? We had fun, and there was laughter, but mainly our existence was about survival and mundane worries. We were void of the human connection, and that's what I needed and wanted most.

The outside was a vast playground for me. I felt naturally free and happy being alone or roaming about in nature. The affection I wanted from Mama and Papa I found by wrapping my skinny arms around trees, hugging them as much as I wanted—and it felt good. I was starving for love, but a part of me didn't think I deserved it. These were internal thoughts and limiting beliefs of *I am not worthy*. It would take me a long time to discover that not only was I worthy, but also that I am the creator of my own reality.

Over time, my love of the outdoors continued to evolve so much so that I could hear nature calling to me, "Come to

Mama." And off I'd go, often climbing to the top of a mango tree to lie on one of its thicker branches and, maintaining my balance, pick the delicious mango to eat while staring into the sky, daydreaming. The sweet, tropical aroma could put me to sleep if I let it. When I'd climb high enough to see the lush, faraway landscape, I absorbed the most incredible views of paradise. I even made walking three miles to grade school a bit of an adventure. I took whatever path my impulse directed me to, taking shortcuts through streams or sometimes crossing a well-worn bridge. Regardless of my route, I couldn't resist climbing fruit trees. I'd pick the best to eat while using my worn shirt like a hammock to carry an assortment of fruit to school. These I'd sell so I could buy snacks or bribe the teacher if I was late. Kids bullied me in school. I couldn't bother Mama because she was busy with the farm and Papa was working. Except for one time when Sissy stood up for me, I mostly had to fend for myself.

From a young age, I was a free spirit. I loved feeling unconstrained, even with regard to clothing. Mama scolded me for not wearing dresses and skirts and implored me to be more proper like my sister, but it never took. I was a tomboy, choosing to wear shorts over skirts. I loved riding the water buffalo when it pulled the plow to turn the soil. Straddling a buffalo wasn't comfortable in a dress. Besides, at that age, I looked like Mowgli from *The Jungle Book*, and Mowgli didn't like to wear clothes, so Mama was lucky I wore shorts and tops at all.

Maybe I refused to wear a dress because it went against what Mama wanted. I don't know if she was aware of it, but I harbored a deep, unreconciled resentment toward her. She was Mama, our protector because Papa was away working all the time. But she was also the one who gave me away to a relative when he came to get me. He worked out this whole speech, warming up my mother, and then he'd nod at me with a creepy smile and say, "I want to take her with me. She can spend the night." And Mama complied without sensing my fear or questioning why a grown man wanted a little girl for the night. That relative was the most educated in our family. He had gone to college, played the guitar, and regularly attended church. No one questioned him. Even the adults in his house didn't ask why he was around a third grader. To everybody else, he could do no harm, but what he did to me desecrated my young soul. Every time he tried to shove his banana in me, his gooey spunk between my thighs was a searing reminder of his harm on my soul. Sometimes, he'd blindfold me and make me play the guitar, causing further trauma because I didn't know what my uncle was doing or what he would do to me. Seeing him created indescribable fear. If he was present, I was frozen mentally, physically, and emotionally. I couldn't go to Mama or Papa, so I fell into a silent, dark pit, wondering if I was going to get pregnant. I was still a baby, so what would I do with a baby? My uncle stole what little value I thought I had, and each time he sexually molested me, the only thing I could do was bottle up my anger. I felt I was the only one it happened to in the whole world—that I did something I was being punished for, because he continued until I was in the fifth grade. But my uncle wasn't the only one who caused that seed Grandfather planted to grow, forcing me to find a way to the other side of the mountain.

Another one of my relatives treated me just the same. When he'd stay at our house or when we went to my aunt's place, all the kids slept in one bed. That relative made a habit of slipping his hand inside my shirt, groping me. He didn't see me as a person with feelings—a human being. He was an animal. Yet even an animal may have been more humane. Sleep wasn't comforting when I had to worry about my abusive relatives crawling next to me, forcing their hard penis between my thighs. My other family members seemed fast asleep, but I didn't know if they'd done it to them too.

Playing a game of hide-and-seek with our family and friends wasn't what it should have been; I had to fight off that person then too. He'd isolate me and then try to rape me as if it was normal. Was it though? As time passed, I wondered if other girls or women in the village were sexually assaulted, disrespected, and devalued too. If they were, I prayed they, too, had someone in their lives who gave them reason to believe there was something outside of our village, far beyond the mountain ridges they could see.

When I was alone or making Mama's bed, I'd bury my face in her pillow to take in her scent. It gave me a temporary unconditional comfort from what I was holding inside. I could cry or scream, and it didn't yell at me. I think there were times, subconsciously, I made myself sick to get Mama's comfort, hoping it would erase the pain, but that didn't work. My beautiful Mama would look at me crossly and say, "Look, you have to pray and get better!"

◇◇◇◇◇◇◇◇◇◇◇◇

My parents wanted us to get an education, but schooling options were limited in our barrio, so my parents rented a tiny cubicle in a town that offered more opportunities, forty-five minutes away from our village. The cubicle was like a boarding house, but barely even ten feet wide. It had enough room to fit bunk beds, cabinets, a sink, and a hot plate with a small table for six of us elbow to elbow and a little room to wiggle around. My older sister and brother went to trade schools, and I talked Mama and Papa into allowing me to go to Saint Vincent's College, which went from kindergarten through twelfth grade. Several of my classmates talked about going to nursing school. The Philippines being the leading exporter of professional nurses to the United States, it was a guaranteed ticket to go to the most desirable country, but nursing wasn't for me. I fainted at the sight of blood. Plus, my parents couldn't afford nursing school. Still, I was determined to find another way to go abroad. While I was at Saint Vincent's, my relative would come to town and try to fondle me. Though I still lacked the courage to tell anybody about what he was doing, I was a little older now and felt that I could refuse his advances. Finally, he left me alone.

During my first year of high school, writing pen pals became my favorite hobby. Initially, I'd written to a few people my age to improve my English, but there was something special about getting a letter from a foreign land. I found it fascinating to learn about countries where people spoke different languages, had unique perspectives, told stories I'd never heard, and practiced various ways of living. I'd press against my nose envelopes with stamps and seals from different postal regions around the world to smell the possibilities of what the letter went through before reaching my hands. I didn't have money to buy envelopes, so I took pieces of paper and made them myself.

I saved what little money I could scrounge for postage, and I was creative in getting it. Mama had to pay tuition for every exam I took in school. It was my job to remind her when the fee was due, so I began quoting her a slightly inflated amount, which gave me enough money for postage. It was a bit of trickery, but I justified it by being very honest in all other financial matters. I desperately needed a new pair of shoes in high school because my old ones were too worn. I saw a pair in one of the shops in town, but I couldn't afford them. At most those shoes cost a hundred pesos—equivalent to two dollars—but that was a lot to us. I dreamed about those shoes, but I waited for Christmas-time when Papa was getting a bonus before mustering the courage to ask for them. For the most part, I knew better than to ask because things were tight. Between the farm, the cubicle, and four children there were always expenses. I learned to live without a lot of things. Kids at school could rush to the bakery during recess and get their snacks, but not me. Luckily, my best friend was so generous that she'd share her snacks with me. And when we had to buy our books, I didn't bother Mama; my friend shared those too.

That a piece of paper in an envelope could travel from country to country set my mind in motion. If a letter could do that, why couldn't I? America was burning in my brain. I didn't know how I would afford it, but I wasn't going to let that stop me.

◇◇◇◇◇◇◇◇◇◇◇◇

Attitudes toward sexuality and gender are so strongly tied to religious beliefs. I was confused and ridden with trauma from religious conditioning. Even though unspoken, certain things weren't allowed. There was a trans woman in the village who was friends with nearly everybody, and she always wanted me to walk with her. I didn't see anything wrong with it. One time, we went to a festival together. Mama saw us and her expression let me know in no uncertain terms that this type of friendship wasn't acceptable.

In my fourth year of high school, I met Taylor, an exchange student from Washington who went to Saint Mary's, a nearby school. I was immediately smitten. *A girl from America!* We became friends. Taylor was also a tomboy and adventurous. She was in the Philippines for only a year, but I loved that she didn't discriminate against me because I wasn't like the rich kids in our school. I was pleasantly surprised that Taylor took the initiative to find out where I lived and come visit. We hung out often, walking miles along the coast. Taylor didn't tell her host parents about these outings, and I felt responsible for her, although I didn't tell her we really shouldn't be doing those things. I took her to my village in the mountains to show her where I lived. To get there, we crossed a couple of gulfs. The water was waist high and the current rough. There were crocodiles, but we weren't worried about them. We were having so much fun together. But when it was time to return, we encountered a problem. The bridges were flooded, and everything was shut down. I thought Taylor could just stay with us in the barrio, but Sissy insisted that I had to get her back. "You have to walk her to the city tonight," she said, and I did.

We held hands in the ferocious current while crossing the bridge and struggled to find the rail. When we finally reached the main town, we caught a bus so that Taylor could make it back to her host family before they worried. Taylor was smart, very pretty in a boyish way with shoulder-length, curly, light brown hair that she often wore in pigtails. I loved her athleticism and that she played soccer. She loved U2 and was the one who introduced me to music. Taylor was the first person who recognized me—for me.

I didn't have money to buy Taylor anything for her birthday, so I drew a picture of a foot kicking a ball—and she loved it! Sometime later, she invited me to her room. Glancing around, I said to myself, *Wow, she really loved that picture. It's not even in her room.* As if she read my thoughts, she told me to lay down—the drawing was on the ceiling.

Taylor asked me to do a pencil portrait of her and her little brothers. She had five, and she was the only girl. I presented her with the portrait, and she loved it. She asked me to sign my name, so I took the pencil and signed *Lucia*, my birth name, even though I never liked it. That was the name I was given. I hadn't yet discovered the name I would give myself. Taylor pressed twenty dollars into my hand. I tried to refuse, but she insisted. "I'm paying you for this," she said. I had never been paid for anything I'd done.

When Taylor returned to America, she carried that portrait on the plane with her. My experiences with Taylor made me feel something other than invisible. She noticed and invested time in me, which was overwhelming. Taylor made me want to get out of there because she took me away from the bad and everything that had happened to me. When she left, it was like someone was ripped out of my heart, and I didn't know how to handle it. I realized I'd fallen in love with Taylor.

◇◇◇◇◇◇◇◇◇◇◇◇

I went to the library to read about America and its different regions—something about California tickled my fancy. A girl sitting next to me was reading through a thick medical textbook, probably studying something to do with nursing. However, the white pamphlet lying next to the medical book caught my attention.

The girl turned to me and asked, "Would you mind watching my stuff while I go to the restroom?"

I nodded and said, "Sure."

As the girl got up and left, I reached over and picked up the pamphlet. I couldn't peel my eyes off it. It was a list of American bachelors searching for Filipino wives. I scanned the list, checking out the photos next to each profile. I didn't realize that the girl had returned from the restroom and was standing behind me.

"Are you interested?" she asked.

Startled and slightly embarrassed, I shrugged. "Maybe." But my excitement got the best of me. "Are you writing to any of the Americans?" I asked, beaming with curiosity.

"No." She shook her head as though the thought never crossed her mind. "I'm too scared. What if it doesn't work out and you're far away from your family? I heard about this girl who left to marry her pen pal, and she found out the guy had thirteen jars in the basement, one of them empty."

"What are the jars for?" I asked with a light giggle.

"Thirteen jars with women's heads in them and one's empty. What do you think the empty jar is for?" She insisted the anecdote was true. "Somebody told me they heard the story."

"Sounds like something you see in the movies," I said, dismissive of her warning. I wasn't afraid. "You doing nursing?" I continued.

"Premed."

"You got options. Some people don't. Do you mind if I borrow this?" I asked, tapping on the list of bachelors.

"It's actually my aunt's. She'll be so upset if she finds out I stole it."

"Okay, I'll just write down five of them. I like the California ones."

I copied the information down as fast as possible in case the girl ran out the door with that fancy list.

I began corresponding with the Americans in the middle of my senior year. My communication was direct. I told each of them: *I am writing because you want a wife. It's a given that you are going to get me out of here. I am coming to America to be your wife, and you will provide for me. This is the deal.* I'd graduate in March of 1989, and I planned to be on my way to America by then, at the mature age of seventeen. I never discussed my aspirations.

Had I said anything, my family would have tried to talk me out of it. Nobody I knew was a mail-order bride. Still, I had to forge my path.

I was nowhere near understanding what I was willingly entering into, but I looked at the prospects as men who earned a living, provided, and ran the house and family. I didn't see them as middle aged or old. They were providers and protectors, which was something I didn't have. My refuge was in my head, over the mountain ridges. I thought whoever I married would look out for me and be someone I could go home to. This decision was about survival. I had no connection to my feelings. I was merely drifting on autopilot.

If the men were desperate enough, they sent their reply by express mail, but ordinarily it took about six weeks to receive replies. The postman walked door to door in town delivering mail. I always kept a look out for him to keep Mama or anybody else from intercepting my letters. Out of the five letters, I received three replies. One came from San Francisco, another from Las Vegas, and the last from San Diego. All three of them were good looking, financially secure, loving, affectionate, romantic, *blah blah blah*. Harvey, the San Francisco guy, was attractive, but that wasn't a major consideration. I was still in survival mode, making my decisions from that vantage point. He stood out because he enclosed dollars to cover the postage cost, and he wrote on luxury stationery.

In six months of writing, I received five letters from Harvey. When we decided to communicate by phone, I traveled five hours by bus to get to the closest long-distance telephone station. Without any prodding, he decided to come to the Philippines to see me. I still hadn't told anyone about my plan, but I knew I had to tell my parents that some sound engineer guy from California was coming. What an awkward and uncomfortable thought. My parents had never seen me interact with a guy. I didn't know why, but until Harvey, I'd shrink in utter embarrassment if one had.

The year 1989 was a dangerous time in Manila, especially for foreigners. There was a massive coup d'état in Manila, where Harvey would first land. Allegations of human rights abuse, political turmoil, and mass corruption led to the People Power Revolution, and our president, Ferdinand Marcos, was in the process of being overthrown. Fighters bombed a couple of places; flights were canceled, and chaos ensued. Harvey had to get through Manila to get to Dipolog City—that's *if* he got on a flight and *if* they didn't blow up the plane. I figured if he made it to my town, then he was the one. Even though Harvey told me when he was due to arrive, there was no way for me to find out ahead of time if he got on the flight. All I could do was go to the airport and wait for him to show up.

I went alone to meet him so my family wouldn't waste their time trying to talk me out of being a mail-order bride. Everyone I knew was afraid of the unknown, which is why they made sure I stayed in the known. Only I was certain *the unknown*, that place of fear, held freedom and possibilities beyond my imagination. The known gave me the creeps and scared me, so I wasn't letting the opportunity escape me.

His flight landed. I watched the passengers descend out of the small aircraft, and there was Harvey. Standing out, he was about six foot three, blond, and handsome. My God! I thought to myself, *I hit the jackpot!* It was like James Bond landed in town on an extraordinary mission. Thirty-three years old, blue-eyed, and sophisticated, he had this guise that made him seem unapproachable, but he could be if I had what he needed. Harvey towered over everybody, and not just physically; his appearance commanded attention without even trying, partly because he was Caucasian and stood out like some godsend authority on a small remote Philippine island with limited diversity.

Harvey looked slender and fit with healthy glowing skin, his hair gelled back, and wearing light blue striped dressy trousers, a white long-sleeve button-down shirt, and a fresh pair of vintage-style Nike sneakers. Harvey was squeaky clean. His pink and red face was tight, wrinkle free like he just stepped out of a skin-care salon after having a perfect face-lift. I mumbled, "This guy *is it* from head to toe—and he chose me."

Harvey spotted me right away, black hair down the middle of my back, five foot two, wide-eyed, and perched on an elevated platform to be a little higher than his waistline; otherwise, it would have been incredibly awkward. Sizing him up as he walked toward me, everything about that man was perfect. At least—with my wonderful imagination, I made him that way.

"Hello."

"Hi," he replied, with a warm smile, towing a large piece of luggage with a carry-on draped across his right shoulder.

"We have to get a cab to take us to the hotel," I told him.

"Okay. After you," Harvey said, allowing me to lead the way.

Our conversation was about logistics. I never had a boyfriend, didn't interact with guys on a romantic or personal level, and I was only seventeen—all of this was new. We knew what we were there for, making it awkward to talk. I didn't know what to say to him because there was no connection, and I wasn't conscious of how this contractual thing would go now that we were face to face. But the way he looked at me made me feel like I stood on a pedestal, and I quickly found myself in a different state of existence. Perhaps he was a hologram that would disappear in a snap because I kept asking myself, *Is this for real? This must be love. Who knows?* When Harvey's scent wafted up my nostrils, it made me forget he was a total stranger. He wrapped his arms around me, pulling me inside his embrace as though I was already his. A momentary sense of relief flooded my body, but it dissipated when the reality of telling my family about Harvey hit me. After the first hug, I stepped back while my mind freaked out. How would I explain him to my parents?

Nobody knew I was leaving, and I never tried to fully understand why I was fleeing. All I could think of was running away from everything and everyone before processing why. Part of me felt that I was doing something wrong, giving me no reason to broadcast my planned escape. Besides, I didn't want to occupy my mind with their concerns, and I certainly didn't want to hear my own. I became a mail-order bride to rescue myself, so I blocked everyone out. No one could sway my decision since they couldn't even save me while I was here, right in front of them, hurting. I had to look out for myself before something else happened.

Harvey must have wanted a wife pretty badly because a bridge was bombed in our city and things were much worse than in America, but he dealt with the political unrest by working around it. Harvey openly confessed that I wasn't the only girl he came to see; three of us were his top picks. He'd visited the first two girls in the northern part of the country, but Harvey told me that I was the most innocent-looking girl. The others were from the city, and he thought they were too clever for him. Harvey was looking for someone naive and fresh that he could mold to his desire—and I fit the role perfectly.

◇◇◇◇◇◇◇◇◇◇◇◇

The resort sent representatives to pick us up from the airport in Dipolog City and take us to an exclusive and romantic beach resort thirty minutes outside of town. The discrete location shaped like a horseshoe was tucked away in the mountains and accessible only by boat. From what I could tell, it catered primarily to foreigners. Harvey liked the exclusivity.

We stayed in bamboo villas. Most locals also had bamboo-made homes or "huts," but the opulence and decadence of the villas was worlds away. The villas were spread out, each with a private path connected to multiple swimming pools, a bowling alley, a disco bar, banquet and recreational centers, a mountain-top chapel, and a kiosk where you could rent equipment for the beach.

Lunch at the cabana close to shore was our first meal together. Watching the calm waves gave me a sense of realness to the surreal moment. It was strange to be waited on by people of my kind wearing neatly pressed, perfectly tailored uniforms. I felt extremely awkward wearing a bathing suit and walking side by side with Harvey because all eyes were on me. I couldn't help but wonder what people thought of me with the American. They could tell I was fresh out of high school. I imagined some of them were envious. They would've had to scrounge college degrees to earn those impeccable uniforms and work in a place like this, but I'd not only found a shortcut inside—I was also a guest. The difference between me and the staff was tangible. I got to enjoy the lavish life while they had to serve me. Though I enjoyed the luxury of the hotel, I was uncomfortable throughout the stay.

Harvey doted on me, opening doors, pulling out my chair, and waiting until I took my seat before he sat down. His calm demeanor, probably exhausted from making it through the bombing, made me feel safe. After lunch, we went bowling and Jet Skiing. He even let me drive. I cranked up the speed too fast and lost control, throwing both of us off. As we swam back to the Jet Ski, he leaned in so close to me, I thought I was going to drown in his carbon dioxide. My heart pounded not so much because he kissed me for the first time, but at the thought that there was no turning back at this point. *That's it, girl! He's got you!* I had nothing to compare his kiss to, so I didn't know how I felt about it. I wished I had an instruction book on what to do instead of winging it and flinging myself over the mountain ridges without knowing where I was landing.

I left Harvey alone at the resort while I went home to process the day's excitement. The next day, I returned to the resort with an acquaintance. Her father was the captain of my village. In our impoverished remote barrio, her family was considered wealthy. She wasn't a friend I could share anything with, but I thought this girl would trade her soul to be able to see this scheme of mine. She was relatively sheltered and would never do anything close to what I was doing. She was eager to be a fly on the wall, and I trusted her discretion. Having someone bear witness reassured me somewhat of my newly discovered sanity.

Harvey was anxious to have a lovely gourmet breakfast with me. He was so excited, I saw the spark in his eyes—or perhaps he just had a good night's rest. Over a delicious breakfast, Harvey told me about the dream he had the night before. He took dreams seriously. I noticed a blue and white book of dreams on his side table and I thought Harvey was superstitious for an American.

"Last night, I had a dream that I picked you up at the airport in a limousine." He reached for my hands and added, "Let's say we get married. We start the immigration process now. It'll take six months to get all the paperwork together, then we'll get married as soon as you come to California. If you change your mind during this process—let me know and we'll call it a day. What do you say?"

I would have said, "Fuck, yes!" but at the time, I didn't know such a word existed. I was raised as a strict Catholic, very religious, but this was my long-awaited out and I was going! I accepted.

After his somewhat of a proposal, we went bowling and then relaxed at the resort. It was serene—almost boring, but in a luxurious way. Here I was with the American—and in love. Although far removed from understanding what that meant, it was exciting. When he slipped the ring on my finger, it never occurred to me to ask Harvey anything about himself. I was okay with whatever he brought to the table because my table was empty. Outside of the work people did in the village or Dipolog City, I didn't know what else there could be to Harvey, so I really didn't know what to ask.

◇◇◇◇◇◇◇◇◇◇◇◇

That evening, I mustered up some courage to tell Mama and Papa about Harvey. When I went home, I walked up to Mama and held out my hand, displaying the gold, crown-like engagement ring. A visible shock wave hit. I could almost see her brain recalibrating as I told her about the American and my plan to move abroad.

"You don't know anyone in America," Mama proclaimed in our Bisaya dialect.

She was right. I didn't. But I made my decision and felt unless anyone had something encouraging to say, I wanted them to keep it to themselves. No one I knew had gone to America or done what I was attempting because the thought of it was unimaginable to most people. Not to me though. When life in the village pushed me in the direction of finding myself on my own, I inhaled as much air as my lungs could handle and breathed life into my vision.

Papa couldn't even look at the ring. He just listened to what I said with his eyes closed. But that was his usual demeanor. Papa was quiet, never really saying much. We knew when he meant something just by the look on his face.

I showed Mama photos of Harvey, and I've never seen her look so intently at someone's picture.

"He's awfully handsome," Mama admitted. "But why does he have to travel this far, to this remote part of the world, to find a wife?"

I didn't know what to say. I never thought of it like that. *Who cares? I need to get out of here*, I thought to myself.

Before they could recuperate from the initial heart attack, I dropped the rest of the bomb.

"I'm leaving for Manila next week to process my fiancée visa. Then from Manila, I'm flying to San Francisco, California. Harvey's going to arrange everything for me and send me money. So it's not going to cost you anything. Not a penny."

There was a long deafening silence. I'm pretty sure my father died at that very moment. He was a dedicated father who did his best to provide for us, and I loved Papa for that. He seemed to work 24-7 because we rarely saw him at home or in bed. Mama, on the other hand, was extremely frustrated. I harbored a deep resentment toward Mama, and I sensed her growing discontentment with what she perceived her life to be, trivial and devoid of anything remotely deserving of recognition. I resented her for making herself so insignificant because that's where I learned to be small and unimportant. Now I had to work super hard to unlearn all that crap! Where would I even begin?

Mama processed as much as she could in those few minutes. Making quick decisions wasn't her thing, and she usually took the time to think about something, pray on it, maybe even do a novena for the right decision to come. And *novena* means "nine successive days." If I left this to her to decide, I would turn into mold. But I could feel it coming; she reached a verdict.

"You have never been to America. You have never even been to Manila, and you don't know anyone there," she lectured with a detectable air of concern.

Everything that came out of my mother's mouth translated to the big "No." It's not even that she told me no. I don't think she knew what she was saying because Mama operated in such a negative sphere that everything seemed like an impossibility, regardless of the situation. I couldn't help but feel choked up in her negative vibration, and she couldn't help herself either. Through the years, I'd suffocated and drowned in her negativity. Her mama and papa passed a golden baton of impossibility, and Mama tried desperately to force it into my hand, but I refused. I just wanted to explode like a hand grenade with the pin pulled. The thought of what was behind the mountain ridges was the beginning of a new life. Grandfather planted the strongest seedling, and as it grew, so did that vision, and it catapulted my desire to see what was on the other side of this life. I was fighting to break the blind cycle of acceptance by first understanding what it was I was accepting—and then ensuring that it resonated with me.

For the first time, I talked back to my mother. "Well, Mama, this would be a good time to hook me up with your connection with the big guy," I said with such grace.

And, for the first time, I felt like a grown-up person. Mama actually took it well, and by the end of the conversation, I made it clear that I was leaving, and no one was going to stop me. I took full responsibility for my actions, so they knew I wouldn't blame anyone other than myself if anything went apeshit.

After all of that, Papa still hadn't uttered a word. He went mute. I appreciated his silence. It was the most honest and supportive he could have been at that moment. It was his version of giving me his blessing, and I took it as a gift. He didn't oppose my leaving. He understood. At one point Papa had to do the same thing. He went to a different town to survive; I was going to a different country. Papa was a quiet man, not very opinionated, and I felt he was trying to process what was going on in my head. When I finished explaining everything, we didn't hug or anything. He probably wondered what had happened to me. Just as well, Mama had enough to say for both of them.

That night was excruciatingly uncomfortable because my family never discussed things. It wasn't that we didn't want to; it wasn't in our system. The exchanges were pretty much about checking boxes on our daily assigned chores. Despite everything going on in my confused brain, I felt I had nothing to say to anyone, including myself. Seeing Harvey those couple of days gave me a sliver of hope and enough confidence to muster up the courage to tell my parents without asking their permission. It was more of a declarative statement—I had taken control of my freedom!

I'm pretty sure my parents didn't sleep that night. I didn't either. I was wide awake, feeling the pride of finally speaking up for myself, and I felt alive. Possibilities were swirling in my head with the excitement of how I could finally get out of that suffocating little box and into the arms of America. In the dark, I stared closely at the slight shimmer of the gold ring Harvey put on my finger. Tomorrow, back at the resort, my ass will be waking up next to this guy. I remember this heavy feeling of a death sentence looming over me in concrete imprisonments for a crime I didn't commit or worse, for no apparent reason. I bottled it all in until I punctured a needle-sized hole through the thick concrete wall to feel the sliver of hope again. I went from standing still to stepping on the accelerator full throttle going 110 miles per hour. I quickly revved up the engine. For better or worse, I was going to America.

Before Harvey returned to America, I introduced him to my parents over a very solemn lunch. My siblings came, too, but they were just flies on the wall. Harvey—thirty-three years old, tall, blond, and handsome—officially asked for my hand in marriage. For a traumatized seventeen-year-old, that's awkward as fuck! I told Harvey how my family was religious, especially Mama. But he had a solution for that; he handed Mama an envelope of money as a dowry or church donation, promising he'd take good care of me and send me to school in California. This guy did everything right. He made himself appear like a saint! When lunch was over, Mama was awestruck; she saw Harvey with a halo. Well, at least that's how she came to terms with the idea of her daughter with a stranger.

"He's not so bad. This whole thing is not such a bad idea," Mama confessed.

◇◇◇◇◇◇◇◇◇◇◇◇

There was a deep feeling of disconnect, a sense that I was far removed from everybody, even myself. Mama had never sat down with me and asked how I was doing or talked to me about anything personal she thought I would need to know. She hadn't even spoken to me about my vagina or what I was supposed to do with it. Mama mostly lectured us, reading parables from the Bible and how we should always fear God. I had to confess my sins every week. I was indoctrinated into thinking that I was a sinner. My response was to commit sins so I could go to confessions weekly to fulfill the godly duty.

Growing up, I often got sick from asthma attacks or bronchitis, usually something to do with my lungs. As I gathered the paperwork I needed to take with me to America, I thought about how illness temporarily garnered Mama's attention. I valued those moments of affection, even if they didn't last long. Mama quickly got fed up with attending to me. Amid my convulsive coughing, she would say, "You are just gonna have to decide to get well because I can't do it anymore."

The starvation for Mama's love and affection was profound. Coupled with the inability to get her attention, it made me feel neglected as a child, creating a more profound sadness. Being the third child of four, I thought I had to be the oldest or the youngest child to get Mama's attention; otherwise, I wasn't important, just an extra. I felt insignificant and that there was no reason for my existence in the barrio. I authorized those thoughts. I signed off on them. Now, I had the opportunity to find what I'd been searching for all along.

I was cognizant that I was running away, and even though I believed it was the most sensible way to protect myself from the truth about my life, I still felt guilty. The day I left, I couldn't look my family in the eyes. But there was no looking back. At seventeen, I had to build the muscle between my ears to deal with myself before I could begin to deal with anybody else. I had to develop that muscle on my own—no machines, no gym memberships.

There were so many painful memories that I can't recall how I said goodbye to my family, but I do remember that I buried my face in Mama's pillow one last time and inhaled her scent to take with me forever. My mind must have hop-skip-jumped over the rest. The memories are there somewhere; I must have put them in the recesses of my mind. Trying to survive, I learned that skill.

◇◇◇◇◇◇◇◇◇◇

Before America, I first had to go to Manila to begin the immigration process. I left around Easter. Typically, we didn't do anything at that time of year other than atone for our sins and go to church; it's sinful to travel or do anything else—a no-no! But I wasn't going to wait. I left the barrio feeling like I had a voice for the first time. Leaving was an opportunity for me to navigate my destiny. Besides, I was being compelled to go. I don't mean by Harvey—he was merely the vessel for my journey. It was my grandfather who gave me the imagination to fly and transcend life, and the Universe was saying to me it was time: "Fly, baby, fly."

2.

I Do?

HARVEY ARRANGED FOR ME TO STAY IN MANILA TO process my fiancée visa, which took a few months. Besides the clothes I had on and the documents I needed, I left home with nothing. The flight to Manila was the first time I'd ever boarded an airplane. It was tiny, but I didn't mind because it got me one step closer to my new life in America. While in Manila, I stayed at a few different places, including pension houses. The immigration people Harvey connected me with had arranged for me to stay with a local family while I awaited my immigration interview, but when the host's daughter got chicken pox, I moved to a hotel. I couldn't get sick, or the government would have denied my immigration status. I felt safer at a hotel anyway.

My mother was right—I was in the big city, and I didn't know anyone. Harvey had given me money to get some of the things I needed, including a wedding dress, while I was in Manila. When I went into one of the little tailoring shops and had a dress made, I found speaking my language caused people to look at me like I was from the country. Even when I asked for my room key, the receptionist gave a discriminating, judgmental stare before cutting her eyes at me as she looked to see if I actually had a reservation.

She quipped, "Who may I ask is the guest?"

I wanted to shout, "Mowgli is here! Mowgli is the guest!" but instead, I answered, "Me. I'm the guest."

The receptionist was hesitant to hand me the key, as though I couldn't possibly be staying in their fancy hotel. I soon learned that slapping them with English got their attention, so after that, I began speaking only English. The time I spent writing my pen pals was already paying off.

People thought I was Black and teased me because of it, but when I spoke English, they suddenly treated me like my skin was lighter and stopped thinking of me as a country girl. I dreamed in English and articulated thoughts more fluently in English than in my language, which I thought lacked the depths of ideas and opinions I needed to express to others. All along, I was preparing for my journey.

◇◇◇◇◇◇◇◇◇◇◇◇

I was in awe of how gigantic the plane to San Francisco was. As I stared out the window, I couldn't fathom how such a big piece of metal could soar over the mountains. But it did, and quite smoothly. It was the first of what I assumed would be many miracles coming my way in the land of milk and honey.

In the seat next to me was Jake, a ten-year-old Filipino American traveling alone. What kind of parents let their ten-year-old travel alone on a thirteen-and-a-half-hour flight? Mama nearly had a fit that I was traveling at all. We started talking, and he spoke English very well. The way words rolled off his tongue caused me to think he must have spoken a dozen different languages—and it wasn't just the words that came out; it was the thought he put into his words. Jake spoke, acted, and dressed like a little man. His questions weren't something I'd dare ask anyone; they were so personal. It was intimidating but quite refreshing. I probably would never see him again, but if I did, we'd likely be friends forever. Before landing, Jake gave me his number.

"You should call me. My family has a house in San Francisco. You could come live with me," he said assuredly.

"Thank you," I told him. "If the stranger doesn't come to pick me up, I'll be sure to call you."

"You should call me anyways," he replied kindly.

I didn't know what to think. I felt like I was in an altered reality where things made no sense—in a good way. Jake and I parted at the immigration lines in customs. When he turned and looked back at me, he had an angel's smile—then, he was gone.

I had to wait a long time in line at immigration. When I finally approached the booth, the immigration officer looked at my Philippine passport, then he stared at me with some kind of judgment, maybe uncertainty or doubt. He came out of his glass cubicle and ushered me down the hallway into an enclosed private office. I thought, *Wow, I must be special.*

He placed my travel documents on the desk and told me to have a seat. Then he left the room. My seventeen-year-old brain was swirling with a bunch of "what ifs," but the loudest one was, What if someone made a big mistake letting me on that plane and now they're sending me back? Just then, a man with a serious expression walked in. He took a seat behind the desk, examined my travel documents, and then he released a long sigh and said, "Fiancée visa."

"I'm confused. Is that a question?"

My paperwork had a big stamp in red that read "Fiancée Visa," so why was he asking me that question with such a pissy face? Before responding to his first question, he fired up another one.

"How old are you? Seventeen?"

I felt interrogated and uncomfortable for being treated as though I'd done something wrong. But I told myself, *You're in America now, keep cool.* So I did my best to remain calm, giving him nothing other than the truth because I'd done nothing wrong.

"Yes."

"How did you meet your fiancé?" he asked.

"At the airport," I said. "That's where I met him for the first time."

"Before that, how did you know each other?" he asked, folding his arms across his chest.

"I saw his name on a list, so I wrote to him, and he wrote back. We were writing for about six months. Then he came to see me."

"How long did he stay?" he asked.

"Three days," I said, fidgeting with my top, wondering if he'd found something to send me back to the village.

"Three days?" he repeated as he scribbled something on the paper.

"I have pictures," I offered. I thought things were not going well. I took a stack of photos out of my carry-on suitcase and handed them to him. I gave him the guided tour as he flipped through half of the photos of our first lunch, when we were bowling, Jet Skiing, and some with my family. He handed the photos back to me, totally unimpressed, like he'd seen them before, even better ones. Then he looked at me funny.

"I'm sending you back," he said, rather routinely.

I'm no dummy. I read people without even trying. This man thought I was a fraud. He'd seen the mail-order bride pamphlets. He'd seen people like me before—people trying to marry their way into America—and it was his job to block us.

"There's a flight back tonight," he said sternly, confirming to me that I was going back immediately.

"I don't understand."

"You're going back. What's to understand?"

I'd come too far to give up that easily.

"But he's outside waiting for me!" I shouted and quickly opened the box I was carrying to show him the wedding dress I had made in Manila. He didn't respond. "He's outside waiting for me. You can go outside and check! He's wearing a black tuxedo, picking me up in a limousine," I said, even though I didn't even know what a limousine was. "Just like in his dream. Harvey dreamed that he picked me up in a limousine, and we drove straight to Las Vegas to get married. So, if you excuse me, I have a wedding to go to."

He studied my reaction to his threat of sending me back. "Do you love him?" he finally asked.

Now there was an honest question. I didn't know what it meant to love someone romantically, but I knew there was only one right answer.

"Yeah, I love him."

My head was still buzzing from the massive airplane when the immigration officer stamped my visa and let me go. I floated out of his office.

I walked out of the arrival area with my carry-on suitcase and the box with my wedding dress, scanning the curb for Harvey before stepping outside.

All of a sudden, I burst into a heaping sob. It hit me in the gut that I was on the other side of the mountain ridge, where everything looked and felt strangely unfamiliar. The place people dream of is a whole different world. Yesterday, I was in a remote village that no one had heard of, and now, I was on another planet, beginning an entirely different life. No Mama. No Papa. No siblings. No one—except Harvey. The people had different colors and different shades of those colors.

Hardly anything moved in the village, except the grazing buffaloes soaking in the mud. America was the opposite. My nerves were overloaded with stimuli. I felt numb. I didn't have the slightest clue how this place worked. Everyone was hustling, buzzing, and moving. Everything was fast. Just as I felt I couldn't breathe in the barrio, suddenly, America felt the same. I could blame only myself. I took responsibility and said—*Who told you to do this? Nobody! That's right. You're on your own, girl! Show me what you got. This is the other side of the mountain ridge you always dreamed about—the exciting unknown! Explore! Explode! You can always change your freaking mind or get a new one. This is America—anything is possible if you believe.*

I stepped through the double sliding doors.

Harvey looked like a knight in shining armor in his black tuxedo. Of course, he wasn't riding a warhorse, but he stepped out of a black limousine, just like in his dream. Harvey dashed toward me wearing a wide grin like he won the SuperLotto. But he stopped halfway, like someone ripped the smile off his face. Then, sizing me up, sauntering, he came closer.

"You're not wearing your dress!"

"The dress, I have it here," I said, nodding at the box under my arm.

"No, no, no, in my dream, you're wearing the dress when I pick you up."

"Oh, I didn't know I was supposed to wear my wedding dress on the way here." I glanced around for somewhere to change and suggested, "I can put it on now if you want me to?"

"Yes, I want you to go back in there," he said, pointing into the lobby. "Find a bathroom and put your dress on."

It was not a request, so I did as instructed. A moment later, I came back out to find Harvey standing by the limousine. He looked completely stunned when he turned around and saw me wearing a white satin wedding dress with my shoulders exposed. Harvey ran toward me again, but this time he didn't stop. Instead, he swept me up in his embrace and twirled me around as if showing off his trophy. Then, he picked me up and carried me into the back of the limousine like a doll. Inside the limo, it felt like a big funeral vehicle. Seeing everything in black conflicted with what I had in my mind. It made me question if that was the way to celebrate here; did you have to die to get that kind of treatment? Behind the steering wheel was the silhouette of a man wearing a hat. I told Harvey that I wanted to thank the man for taking his time to pick me up even though we didn't know one another.

"You look exhausted. Why don't you get some sleep?" Harvey suggested. "The drive will take a few hours."

Crossing the enormous Golden Gate Bridge blew my mind into such a frenzied daze there were fireworks inside my brain. Everything I saw was giant—the bridge, the city, the houses, the roads, the cars, and even the people! My overloaded system shut down and I fell asleep with Harvey cradling me in his arms.

◇◇◇◇◇◇◇◇◇◇◇◇

"Honey, we're here," Harvey announced, waking me up.

No one had ever called me that name; it sent chills up my spine. I lifted my face from the drool on his black tuxedo's lapel as the limousine pulled up to a wedding chapel. We must have arrived at the best possible time because there was no line. The chapel was in the Guinness World Records for having the most "to-go" weddings in a day.

"Oh wait, we have to go to Las Vegas city hall first," Harvey alerted the driver.

When we arrived at the city hall, I was still out of it. Harvey did all the talking.

The clerk behind the counter asked, "Does she speak English?"

"She does," Harvey said proudly. "She speaks good English."

He went on boasting about how he picked me up in a limousine at the airport.

The clerk winked at me and said, "Beautiful dress," before turning to Harvey, adding, "My, what a beautiful bride you have there."

Harvey beamed with pride as he handed the clerk both of our birth certificates. The clerk checked mine.

The clerk became perturbed. "She's seventeen. She's not legal!"

But Harvey had an answer for that too. He took out a piece of paper from the folder and handed it to the clerk through the window cut in the glass. "I've got both of her parents' consent here."

I thought it funny that after reaching the destination I always wanted, I found myself anxious to go somewhere else. I felt sick to my stomach.

The clerk wordlessly slid Harvey the marriage license, and we headed back to the wedding chapel, still no line.

"If it's in the Guinness World Records, where are all the people?"

"This is Vegas. It's only 8:20 a.m.," Harvey explained. "Everyone's probably hungover."

We entered the chapel and were greeted by two of the most stunning people I'd ever seen. They looked almost fake. I didn't know who they were until Harvey remarked, "There's Elvis Presley and Marilyn Monroe!"

Elvis was the officiant, and I gathered Marilyn was the photographer and everything else as she went to work straightening out my face, throwing on lipstick and a little splash of blush with a few more touches here and there. Smacking her gum, she said, "Smile, dahlin'," so I did because I couldn't look at her and not smile. "Now you're ready," she said, so deliciously.

I wanted to be like her when I grew up. And I wanted whatever gum she was chewing.

"Let's get the show on the road!" Elvis said, calling the shots as the instrumental of "Love Me Tender" played in the background. I walked down the short center aisle with Harvey and stood facing him before Elvis Presley and his perfect hairdo. The music faded and Elvis handed me the ring to put on Harvey's finger.

"Harvey, do you take this beautiful girl as your lawfully wedded wife, from this day forward, for better, for worse, for richer, for poorer, in sickness and in health, until death do you part?"

Oh no—my stomach wanted to jump out of me.

"I do," Harvey said with certainty.

As the words left his mouth, I regretted having eaten a burger on the plane. I was going to vomit. Elvis handed Harvey a diamond ring to put on my finger.

Elvis looked at me solemnly. "Will you take Harvey as your lawfully wedded husband, from this day forward, for better, for worse, for richer, for poorer, in sickness and in health, until death do you part?"

Feeling the barf on the way, I stormed out the door with Marilyn Monroe following behind me. Outside was a large blue planter filled with brightly colored flowers; I bent over and hurled in them while Marilyn Monroe gently rubbed my back in a soothing, circular motion. Instantly, I felt relieved. Handing me a bottle of water, Marilyn dabbed the corners of my mouth with a tissue. I felt dehydrated and chugged the water down. She offered me a tin of gum containing three flavors.

"You like gum?" she asked reassuringly.

I nodded. "Can I have one of each flavor?"

"Have all you want, sweetheart." I took one of each color and popped them in my mouth. We went back inside just as Harvey was coming out to get me.

We returned to Elvis, and he continued, "So, will you take Harvey as your lawfully wedded husband, from this day forward, for better, for worse, for richer, for poorer, in sickness and in health, until death do you part?" Marilyn Monroe snapped several photos from different positions.

I said, "I do?" I didn't mean to, but it came out with a big question mark that I wanted so badly to be acknowledged. But everybody seemed oblivious. I kept chewing the delicious, colorful gum while the groom leaned in and kissed the bride.

After the great vows, off we went, moving on from the other side of the mountain ridge to somewhere over—*the cliff.* Jump. With a parachute. *This is nothing serious.* Nothing I couldn't handle. At least, that's what I told myself.

I'd only seen weddings attended by the entire village; even the uninvited villagers showed up. I wasn't sure what my wedding was, but I assumed I should have been honored that Elvis Presley and Marilyn Monroe were in attendance—even though

I had no idea who they were. I wondered how many weddings with disheveled brides who were nervous, unsure, or barfing she attended every day and how she even got to be Marilyn Monroe. Or was she always Marilyn Monroe? It felt so much better to think of others for a change. It was a good distraction from my insane reality. It made sense that no one was at our ceremony, but I felt a little sad because it was my wedding, seemingly uneventful and unimportant.

After the wedding, Harvey and I took the limousine to Lake Tahoe. At that point, I'd gone comfortably numb. I don't remember much about the hotel, but there was a fancy bed, silky white sheets, big puffy pillows, a shower, and a Jacuzzi tub. As soon as we settled in the suite, Harvey took off his clothes. My God! I had never seen a man naked before in my life! Opening my eyes when my uncle was molesting me never entered my mind.

Here was Harvey perfectly natural walking around with his balls hanging. I was terrified. The sight of them sent me flying straight to the bathroom to hide. I wanted to lock myself in to avoid seeing him naked again. My eyes scanned the bathroom, trying to find ways to preoccupy myself. When I turned on the shower and water sprinkled out, my mouth fell agape. Even in this surreal moment, the wonders of this new country amazed me. Where I came from, I had to use a pail or bucket to douse water over my head while fully clothed. Still, I couldn't keep the shower on for too long or Harvey would think I was drowning and rush in naked. So I brushed my teeth. The fennel toothpaste took my mind off the naked man on the other side of the door.

He knocked on the door.

"Honey, are you okay?"

With a mouthful of toothpaste, I mumbled, "Yeah, brushing my teeth."

I turned off the water and listened, hoping he had walked away from the door. He did. Thank God. I looked around, contemplating what else I could do in there. I knew that eventually, I had to go out and face his hanging balls. But after seeing those things, I had to wonder, what had I done to myself?

For the second time, Harvey knocked.

"Honey, are you okay?" he asked again, sounding a bit worried. But I knew he wasn't worried; he was just anxious for his honeymoon to take off!

"Still brushing my teeth."

"I'm coming in," he said, trying to sound cheerful. He turned the doorknob, but I had locked it. "Honey, it's just you and me here. You don't have to lock the door."

I cracked the door open just a little bit so he could see my mouth was still full of toothpaste.

He opened the door and came in.

"I'm worried about your stomach. Take this," he insisted, handing me a pill. "It's going to make you feel so much better." My stomach was bothering me, but it was because I was processing so much. Still, I swallowed the pill. I wanted to feel better even if only for a moment.

"Why don't you take a bath?" Harvey suggested.

I shrugged.

Harvey just grinned and filled up the tub.

"Relax and enjoy the bath," he said, kissing me on the lips, then he left me alone to bathe.

I'd never taken a bath like that. The pill, whatever it was, swept over my knotted-up nerves. I felt so relaxed, and my teeth felt so clean. After a bit, Harvey cracked the door. "It's not too hot, is it?" Then he stuck his head in and asked, "Why do you have your dress on?"

I was accustomed to bathing in my clothes, but especially

after seeing Harvey and his balls—I wanted to remain covered up! Culture shock hit me hard. I was overwhelmed, without any order of thought, and I wondered again what I'd gotten myself into.

I didn't protest as Harvey helped me undress. I got naked in front of him for the first time. Maybe it was the culture shock or maybe it was the pill, but I felt comfortably disarmed. I couldn't think.

He ran his soapy hands all over my body. The honeymoon was taking off without me. I checked out. I watched Harvey drain the water from the tub. Then he gently dried me off, wrapped the towel around my body, and carried me to the bed. A slight chill hit my skin as he removed the towel and poured oil all over my body. Although it didn't move me, using very sensual strokes, he massaged my body. As I drifted to sleep, I felt his mouth sucking the oxygen out of me.

◇◇◇◇◇◇◇◇◇◇◇◇

I was having a spoonful of honey while gazing at the moon. Our first trip as a married couple wasn't really a honeymoon; it's what Americans call "fishing." We were on a desolate lake, languidly casting lines—Harvey's idea of romance. I wouldn't call that fishing. Where I came from, fishing meant actually catching a fish. What we were doing was merely holding a fishing rod for hours. I was surprised to discover that I was pretty good at it—it calmed my nerves. Holding the rod wasn't the calming part; it was watching the still waters while Harvey was busy reeling, then casting, then reeling it back and casting again and again. I was happy to see him doing something else other than me.

When I looked at Harvey, enjoying the tranquility, a question dawned on me. "Don't you have family and friends? No one came to our wedding."

"Of course! And they're dying to meet my wife." Then, reeling in his fishing line, with nothing on the hook, he excitedly stole a kiss.

As my eyes met the horizon, I sensed a storm brewing. I thought it peculiar to look at Harvey, still a stranger to me and the only person I knew in America—well, other than Jake, but I didn't know where I had placed his number. I barely knew my husband, and he didn't seem interested in learning anything about me. Who I was didn't matter to Harvey because he was going to turn me into whatever he wanted me to be.

I tried distracting myself from a question swelling in my head, but it grew louder—*Who is in charge of your life?* Every fiber of my being had yearned to venture into the unknown. I wasn't in my village anymore, but even after moving to America to marry a stranger, I still didn't feel in charge of my life. My brain had spasms from the overwhelming revelation of what life had thrown at me while exposing my nerves. It became harder not to feel, and the feelings morphed from a gentle whisper into a commanding voice saying, *Wake the fuck up!*

◇◇◇◇◇◇◇◇◇◇◇◇

We were in our hotel room when Harvey handed me a present from his boss's wife, Karena. Even though we'd never met, I was moved by her sentiment and excitedly ripped the box open to find a beautiful green satin dress. Delighted, Harvey watched my face light up as I slipped into it and twirled around. As if handsewn by Mama, the dress fit perfectly. I wondered how Karena knew my size.

Now that the honeymoon was over, Harvey ordered a silver

Lincoln Town Car to take us through a tree-lined, affluent neighborhood in Marin County, just north of the Golden Gate Bridge. The car pulled into a huge three-story house that was festive with loud music playing. Tightly gripping my hand, Harvey led me inside, beaming with pride. As soon as we walked into the room, sedated eyes turned around to look at me. Harvey wrapped his arms around me, showing off his wife as a trophy. The men walked over and congratulated Harvey in the most American way: "You motherfucker!" and "Damn! Ass got brains after all." The most civilized was "Why didn't I think of it?"

Johnny, apparently Harvey's boss, came up and kissed me on both cheeks like a gentleman. Karena stood behind him. She seemed unhappy when I thanked her for the dress.

Most of these people—Karena, in particular—looked at me like a lucky dumb little shit from some remote village. Karena was probably betting everything she had in the bank on just how far I'd go before falling apart. Some of the women in the room looked at me as if they were thinking, *Is this for real?* But a few of them slowly made their way over. They wore expressions of pity, though I couldn't tell if they felt sorry for me or for Harvey. Some discreetly handed me their phone number, urging me to call to get together or chat. I couldn't pinpoint why I felt the kind of chat they envisioned came with a specific subversive agenda. Maybe that's why Harvey watched everyone who came near me like a hawk. When you have a bride fresh off the boat, or plane in my case, first impressions are crucial. The moment anyone spoke to me for more than sixty seconds, he swooped in. He seemed overly protective of his property and didn't want anyone to influence or corrupt my pureness. Preserving innocence is a fundamental element in subservience, especially if you want to mold the perfect sex slave.

My grandmother, bless her soul, never set foot in school, but she was one of the wisest people I'd ever known and taught me to think for myself. She used to tell me, "Use your holy coconut, all that muscle in between your ears the Lord gave you." Now I had to see how I could use the precious coconut the good Lord vested in me.

"Where is the bathroom?" I asked one of the women.

She nodded toward a long hallway. "Second door on the left."

Three middle-aged guys were in front of the door, smoking a joint. To get into the bathroom, I had to weave in between them. One offered me a joint.

Already relatively high, another said, "Hey, that's a beautiful dress. I'm Vince." He extended his hand. "Harvey's my buddy. Do you have a twin sister who wants to come to America?" He looked at the others and chuckled.

"I don't."

Eyeing me quite seductively, the third one said, "Harvey's got it figured out, man. Next summer, I'm going to get an Oriental wife."

"Excuse me," I said politely.

Once they stepped aside, I entered the bathroom while the three of them echoed the exact automated phrase, "Harvey's a great guy," before returning to their joint, which had seeped into my lungs.

By the time I locked the door and emptied my bladder, relieved to have a moment to sit by myself, I overheard the guys talking to Harvey. Of course, he must have followed me. The guys told Harvey that they were splitting.

Then there was a knock on the door. "Honey, you okay?"

I shook my head. What could have gone wrong with peeing?

"Yes, I'm fine," I reassured him, then I heard him walk away.

A moment later, I decided to return to the party before Harvey came back.

I ran into Johnny. "Oh, there you are. Come, my dear, I want to show you something," he said. He ushered me downstairs to the garage where an imposing Rolls-Royce was displayed. He called it a "piece of junk" while caressing it ever so sensually like a delicate geisha.

"Yes, it's a piece of junk," I replied, to be agreeable. Before either of us could say another word, Harvey came down to join us.

"Just showing your wife my precious—" Johnny began, but Harvey cut him off.

"He bought it with *my* money. Ready, honey? We're going home."

He sounded like he was asking me, but it was really a reminder of who was in charge. He shook Johnny's hand, calling him "boss," and we left.

The first time I saw Harvey's apartment I was stunned. It looked like a hurricane had a party of drunken orgies. He claimed that he intentionally kept it that way so nobody would break in. I glanced around and only one word came to mind: *Armageddon*. But there was a silver lining. What I was standing in the middle of would keep me busy while I acclimated to the bigger mess I got myself into. Harvey left me home alone the next day to deal with it. The honeymoon was officially over. I was entitled to lodge a complaint but thought it would be a waste of energy, me complaining to me.

As I separated trash from more trash, I came across a bottle labeled "female attractant." The ingredients included bull's balls. I took a whiff. It was the same scent Harvey wore the very first time I met him at the airport. It all boiled down to that bottle. Apparently, James Bond didn't think he was good enough, so he resorted to some pheromones.

I put the bottle aside and stared at the filthy mess. Even a junkyard was more organized than his apartment. Dirty dishes overflowed in the sink, and his dirty laundry had piled up because he had no time to wash. Junk almost reached the ceiling. There were mountains full of random stuff. I didn't think he knew half the things he had. Compared to the rest of the house, the living room was somewhat decent because there was a little room to move around, although there was no telling what pieces and parts I would step on. The storm was still brewing on the horizon. I was training myself to smell this stink from a mile away. I wasn't paying attention, and that's how I got myself into this mess. I had the feeling that I was back to square one. I wished I could write to my friends and family back home that my life was great in America. But I had to stop lying to myself.

Harvey came home that evening floored at how spectacularly clean everything was; he said it almost felt like home. As a reward, he took me shopping the next day. He didn't have time to stay with me, so he gave me a few hundred-dollar bills, dropped me off at some shopping mall, and told me to meet him in two hours at the same spot. Unfortunately, the mall was overwhelming, and I lost track of time. After wandering around, in some corner of the mall I found a MoneyGram service, where I ended up wiring the money to my family.

I made it back to the spot Harvey dropped me off nearly five hours later, but he wasn't there. I waited and waited, but he never came. I tried to call him from a pay phone, which took me a few tries. When the phone finally rang, there was no answer. It just went to his answering machine. So I decided I'd try to take the bus. I'd never taken a bus that big before, but there's always a first time for everything. My brain was bombarded with having to do everything for the first time. But I tried. I must have gotten on the wrong bus, but I told myself it was okay. Shit happens. I got off on the wrong stop a few times, and after a while,

I decided to stay on and just get off when the sweet lady's shift ended. I could tell she felt sorry for me, and she kindly offered to drive me home. I remembered his address only from writing to him several times.

When I made it home, I couldn't get into the building because I didn't have the key, so I stood by the door waiting. It was pretty late when a guy visiting a resident got buzzed in, and I followed behind him. I knocked and knocked on the apartment door, but Harvey wasn't home. Exhausted, I plopped down on the hallway floor, staring at the door like it was going to swing open until I fell fast asleep.

I didn't recognize the vicious, gnarly dog that shook me out of my sleep. Only it wasn't a dog; it was Harvey. He looked like a wild animal, like he was about to snap my neck.

"Where the fuck did you go!" He grabbed my arm and snatched me up so hard I thought he ripped my arm out of the socket. Harvey shoved me inside the apartment before anybody could hear the commotion.

I didn't think it was possible for someone to be that upset for what I deemed no apparent reason, but once inside, Harvey explained why he was beyond his normal level of anger. To justify his violent reaction, Harvey said, "I'm trying to protect you in case something happens at work. If we have to leave town immediately, you need to be where I can swoop you up and take off!" I looked at him without the slightest idea of what was coming out of his big mouth. He asked where my packages were. The money he gave me was to buy myself some useless undergarments, the heavy-duty erotic lingerie. I told him about wiring the money to my family. Then, big mouth started giving me the lowdown on how sending money to my family was a bad idea. There's a part of me that's always watching as a very keen observer—she makes a career out of observing what's happening while taking copious notes. While Harvey ranted, she paid close attention to his behavior and words. I was in the audience watching this one sad actor in his tragic little play, and I realized that I didn't need to play a part in his dramatic scheme.

3.

A Mother Must Be Born and Reborn

I WENT FROM THINKING, *POOR ME, NOBODY PAYS ME any attention*—to having all of it. Although it wasn't the attention I wanted or needed. Harvey prided himself on micromanaging my life. He decided what I could eat, and what went in and out of my body. Douches and enemas were scheduled on a timely basis, much like a doctor's appointment. Harvey knew when my period was half a day late. And when that happened once, I was immediately given an herbal remedy he got from a friend of his, a Sri Lankan doctor.

A few hours later, I was gripped by a pain so intense that I wanted to bury my head in the sand like an ostrich. Instead, Harvey took me to a macrobiotic restaurant. I could've used some fresh air, but fresh air seemed to evaporate whenever Harvey was around. He sucked it all up. His presence was suffocating.

Once we were seated, Harvey ordered for me. I would have

liked to order for myself and try new things, but he didn't allow it. That time, I didn't care. Whatever he had given me at home rendered me completely out of it. After glancing at the macrobiotic menu, I didn't understand it anyway. All I wanted was white rice, but white rice was among the things I wasn't allowed to have. When the food arrived, I felt a sudden pain clenching my stomach. Excusing myself, I moved as fast as I could, barely making my way to the bathroom. I sat down on the toilet screaming inside and sweating profusely before a huge red blob slid from between my thighs. My heart pounded as I watched it settle in the bottom of the toilet bowl. I wanted to grab it, but I didn't know what to do with it. I stared at it in shock, and tears fell from my eyes.

When I finally got back to the table, I snapped, "What exactly was that pill you gave me? What was it, Harvey?"

"What did you think it was?" he replied dismissively without looking away from his plate.

This clueless little Catholic girl was shaken with the guilt that I had just *killed* something. Although I didn't know what Harvey had done to me, I was sick. And—I was going to hell!

Harvey made it clear that children were out of the question. Whenever he saw kids playing, he said, "They make me uncomfortable. We're not having kids." That was fine with me. Given what I knew about him, I didn't see him and children in the same picture. Still, the thought of what I flushed down the toilet was traumatizing.

◇◇◇◇◇◇◇◇◇◇◇

I wanted to go to school, and Harvey had promised my parents and me that I would go. But his promise wasn't sincere. He'd said what he needed to so that my parents would feel I was in good hands. Now that I was in America, he didn't like the idea of my exposure to the world and all of its deceits that would inevitably corrupt me. He couldn't let that happen. His solution to keeping my mind occupied and me busy was buying me all of the colors of acrylic paints, fine brushes, and the best oak-wood easel money could buy. According to Harvey, I didn't need to go to school; I could simply paint at home in my studio. To make my situation worse, we moved to an isolated house up in the hills. I didn't even see the neighbors and I wasn't allowed to talk to people, including his family, nor was I allowed to make or receive calls. I was completely isolated. This was worse than life in the village. At least there, I had the freedom to socialize and live my own life. Here, I felt like I was marooned on an island in the middle of nowhere.

Finally, I'd had enough. I told Harvey that I was not a hermit, I get cabin fever, and I wanted to work. But he had a lot to say about that.

"Why would you want to work for minimum wage? That's a waste of time. Do you have any idea how much I make?"

"No, I don't. You never told me."

"I make a quarter of a million dollars! That's a lot of money," he added sarcastically.

I didn't know if that was in a day or a year, and I didn't ask. Either way, I never saw any of it. The only time he gave me money was to buy lingerie.

He was a sound engineer, but I was starting to think what he made wasn't legit. I often found big wads of cash under the couch, in cupboards, and buried in weird places around the house. Why couldn't he put it in the bank? He strove to maintain an average and understated image, but when he was drunk and had too much in his head, he'd mumble about trying to keep his shit together. Sometimes when I knew he would be gone for the day, I'd take a little of the money, walk down to the bottom of the hill, and then take the bus to the mall where I could send money to my family. I don't think he ever knew it was gone. Of course, I could have used some of the money for myself, but it would go a long way sending it to them. They needed it more. What I needed was something else.

I could still see the tiny baby that came out of me. Pregnancy had been my biggest fear when my relatives raped me, but I'd never thought about abortion. I never thought that would be me. When I got pregnant again, Harvey didn't give me any herbs. I didn't know what got into him. He never wanted kids. It's not like he suddenly changed his mind. I believed something else was happening; a divine interference was at work, saying this one would be born.

I believe the Universe is held together by a force, a divine intelligence, God, or whatever people want to call it. This intelligence is like the ocean, and humans are like the fish in the ocean. Here comes a clown fish swimming around thinking it's going to the west, but if the ocean current is going north, this clown is heading north, and that's that—divine interference. An unknown force directs the course of events in a way that is beyond intellectual comprehension. What the clown fish believes has no relevance. Its life is sustained and ultimately determined by this immeasurable force. The intellect is the clown fish who cannot see the ocean in its entirety, but it can very much directly experience it by the mere fact that it's swimming in it.

Harvey could not keep controlling things without consequences biting him in the ass. As for me, I was still checked out; I was still not in my body. I felt like a clown fish swimming in all directions looking for the ocean. I was at the mercy of divine intelligence, so I started to pray, *Please, God, if you're going to help me, this would be a good time.* But then, I asked myself,

How do I know God is not already helping me? That moment was an important revelation for me. I suddenly became aware of the connection between myself and the divine intelligence and was vaulted into an elevated state of existence. This clown fish just needed to jump mighty high, suspending in midair just a second longer to see that the mother ocean was cradling her in its arms the whole time.

◇◇◇◇◇◇◇◇◇◇◇

In my second trimester, we had a mandatory appointment with the immigration office for my final interview regarding my status. He quickly reviewed my case folder, then he looked at my unhappy expression. The officer's face turned red as he sized up Harvey towering over me. Without saying a word, he took out a stamp, pressed it hard on a red ink dip, and then slammed it down on the paper. The red ink made a solid six-letter word right on the front page of my documents. DENIED. This meant I would get deported.

Oddly, at this point, I didn't care, but Harvey did. He freaked out. In that short period of being strangely married, I had become the source of his identity, and he was not going to allow his identity to be ripped away from him with that red six-letter word. Thank goodness I was wearing underwear, because Harvey abruptly leaned over and lifted my dress. He pointed to the stretch marks on my tummy.

Harvey and I had one thing in common: we both had distorted perceptions of each other. I thought he would provide a safe haven and be my knight in shining armor guarding me from the boogeyman, but I needed to reframe my thinking since that wasn't happening. I decided I'd be my own knight in shining armor, but one that shines brightly even without armor. Harvey wanted an Asian trophy that he could show off to his fair-weather friends. Someone exotic and subservient to prove he was different and superior. He wanted someone young and beautiful to exude his immortal ego. And most importantly, he was seeking a girl he could mold to his liking. He was so set on his image of a wife that anything threatening to change his picture would send him over the cliff.

I had exhausted myself trying to fight life and fix everything, when all I was doing was running away. Running away from what? *The truth about myself.* Nothing was working, at least, not the way I wanted. But maybe things were not supposed to go the way I wanted. I let out a sigh of relief. If the officer sent me back to the Philippines, then fine.

"My wife is pregnant!" Harvey barked at the officer in a don't-fuck-with-me tone.

The officer shifted to a stoic expression and asked me, "Is this true?" in utter disbelief.

But before I could reply, Harvey assured the officer that not only was I pregnant but that he was proud of it. I sat there thinking, *For Christ's sake, this is not an Oscar acceptance speech.*

The officer opened his desk drawer, took out a different stamp, pressed it hard on a black ink dip, and bam, there it was—APPROVED. I thought the officer merely wanted to get Harvey's American ass out of his face. Which meant I got the privilege of staying in America for good!

◇◇◇◇◇◇◇◇◇◇◇

Working on a six-by-seven-foot acrylic piece on a canvas leaning against the wall of my studio, I felt the intensifying contractions warn the baby was inching its way out. I had never worked with this medium before, but it was easier than oil. I was determined to finish that piece before the baby arrived.

The assistant midwife entered the room, checked my cervix, then she let me return to painting. She sat next to me while I experienced weird sensations in my giant watermelon tummy. When the contractions became stronger, I paused for a moment, feeling I should do something. I was pretty sure it was the baby talking; it was a smart one. I didn't know the sex, but I suspected it was a boy because it kicked so hard I thought he was playing soccer, and my ribs were the goal.

It was Harvey's idea to have a natural birth at home. I thought he was crazy and wanted to write a letter to God that read: *Hey, this man is pretty smart. Is there anybody you can send to show him how to use his brain in a higher frequency, please? Amen. Oh, by the way, I could use one too. Please send a battalion for me. Thank you.*

I told the midwife when I thought it was nearly time to deliver and she called in reinforcements. I couldn't get ahold of Harvey because he had only a pager and I didn't have the number. Per his instructions, I wasn't supposed to page him anyway. Once I knew the other midwives were on their way, I went back to painting. In a pleading tone, I told the midwife that I needed to finish the painting before the baby came. She nodded agreeably and quietly watched me complete the painting without disruption.

My studio was on the second floor of the two-story house, and the birthing tub was downstairs. Finally, the midwife expressed her concern that paint would get all over the baby and insisted that I lay down so she could check how far dilated I was. It took a couple of minutes to do a little touching up, then I was done. Then, as instructed, I went downstairs and climbed into bed, exhausted. When Harvey came home, he began filling the birthing tub for me to get in. I asked for Advil or something to kill the pain.

Harvey snapped, "You can't have any painkillers! This is a natural home birth, bitch!"

"You do it!" I barked back, but only in my head. He could be unpredictable, and I couldn't risk him responding poorly in front of the midwife.

Harvey didn't hold my hand or say a single loving or kind word throughout the birth. He solely focused on the process of the birthing, and that it was happening according to his vision.

I had just gotten in the birthing tub when the head midwife finally arrived, appearing as though she was ready to give birth herself. The pain had intensified, and after hours of soaking combined with the heat, the baby wouldn't come out. I looked over at Harvey and the useless midwives; they were all watching me suffer in incredible pain, with no semblance of sympathy. After shriveling up like a prune, I reassured everybody, mostly Harvey, that I was the one giving birth, and I had something to say about the labor. I laid down while the midwives took turns massaging around my precious vagina. Ah! What a luxury! She told me not to push, but my body wanted to try. They continued massaging me for a couple of hours—but still, no baby.

Twenty hours into labor, we decided to break the water while I was lying in bed. And within a half hour, a feisty, slime-covered baby slid out of the birth canal. My heart pounded and my whole body shivered when I found out my baby was a healthy little girl. I had a feeling that was just the beginning. God was sending a girl to kick my ass! The midwife gently placed her in my arms with the umbilical cord still attached. I was completely overwhelmed by her presence. My daughter stared at me with her piercing eyes like she knew me all too well and was saying, "I hope you have your shit together."

Like a deer caught in the headlights, I thought, *No, I don't! Please don't look at me like that!*

Begrudgingly, I appreciated Harvey's insisting on a home birth. Sure, his motivations were fanatical and self-obsessed, but after holding my little angel—Amelia—I appreciated the intimacy of the arrangement.

The next day was the first day of my being a mother, and I didn't know what that meant. Numb from the labor, I didn't have the chance to figure out what was happening before I noticed I possessed body parts I'd been waiting for—I now had two perfect boobs filled with breast milk, which reminded me that nothing was random. *Everything has a purpose and comes at the right time.*

Now it was Amelia and me. I never thought I'd be a mother, but she was a welcomed detour to this journey without a map. Or perhaps I had intentionally veered off course. I was starting to learn to go with the flow. The hardest part was that I suffered from postpartum depression and had no one to talk to since Harvey was on his own dying planet. Every night, I cried while cradling Amelia in my arms, knowing she must have felt my sadness.

I'd begun to realize I ran away from a hellish pit simply to find myself in another hellish pit. Only now, I was isolated with Harvey in another country. I didn't want to complain because part of me was grateful that my uncle wasn't around. I ran away, hoping those memories would dissolve. Still, no matter how or where I chose to isolate myself, the memories and emotions were dead bolted inside me, confirming I hadn't left anything behind—*I just left*, and all that shit followed. Mentally and emotionally, I hit bottom, then I realized that was okay because I had nowhere to go but up once I got up. I was alone because Harvey wasn't there for me. All he wanted was for me to fulfill my duties as a wife. He couldn't see or have empathy for what I was going through.

Harvey didn't want to be bothered with the baby crying, so I moved to the second bedroom, where I locked myself away with my daughter. It turned out to be a blessing. I didn't want to be around anybody, especially Harvey. I was fine with just Amelia.

Forcing myself to pull it together, I started painting again, this time exploring watercolors, and it worked well for Amelia too. I still cried every night, but having my own room, my own little space, crying was now a release, like my heart was showering and cleansing itself. Subsequently, I'd look forward to crying as a way to comfort myself with the realization that I was running away from home, which I knew, but now at a new level of understanding. Anything I ran away from stayed with me all this time and went wherever I did. I couldn't outrun sadness, pain, trauma, or fear.

Looking at Amelia was equivalent to taking a deeper look at myself. I hoped that we could be good friends and talk about anything. I wanted to protect her like a lioness protects her cub, make her laugh from her soul, and provide the space and type of relationship that would allow Amelia to feel comfortable crying in front of me so I could hold her through those tears. I prayed she would never feel the sadness I had experienced or get hurt and abused the way I did. The hope I had for myself was that I'd get my shit together.

◇◇◇◇◇◇◇◇◇◇◇

On Amelia's first birthday, I baked a carrot cake. It was the first one I ever made. I finished decorating it with icing when Harvey walked in extremely upset. Before saying a word, in a terrifying outburst, he picked up the cake and hurled it across the room. The cake smashed against the wall and broke into bits as it landed on the floor—that's what hurt me. I had poured my heart into that cake—*I was that cake!* It would have been bearable if he had tried to smack my face and left the cake alone. At least I would have been able to duck to avoid his hand. That was the first wake-up call I paid attention to regarding Harvey. Without hesitation, I picked up Amelia. Holding her snugly, I headed for the door. Before I could step out, Harvey grabbed me by the collar, yanking me back, and said, "If you leave me, you are going to be selling yourself on the street!"

That's how little he thought of me and my abilities. I looked at Amelia, asking myself, *How do you feel about that?* I told myself with conviction, that's nonsense. I'm from the jungle. Leaving is a walk in the park. I had nothing, and I'd be leaving nothing. It felt great to remove that fear from my life. Despite his cruel words, Harvey didn't release my collar. He dragged me into the living room and sat me down, ensuring I wouldn't leave. But everything had already changed. After that, I knew I wasn't afraid to go. It was just a matter of finding the right opportunity.

A few days later, the phone rang off the hook, but no one left a message. Harvey routinely screened his calls. Usually, the answering machine picked up, and once the person on the other line started to leave a message, if it was someone Harvey wanted to talk to, he'd pick up the phone. But things were different now. Harvey knew who the caller was—somebody he needed to avoid because they were angry with him. That may have explained why he was drinking so much. After a few days of calls, the mysterious caller finally left a message. Harvey was drinking as he stared at the answering machine, listening. Normally, I stayed out of Harvey's business, but this time, I had a feeling that whatever he got himself into concerned me and my safety as well as Amelia's, so I eavesdropped.

The angry voice was familiar. It was Johnny, sounding like a kid who had just lost his favorite toy (his Rolls-Royce), his expensive house in Marin County, and perhaps his high-maintenance wife, Karena, too. Listening in, I learned that Johnny had been audited by the IRS. Additionally, the recording studio where Harvey was supposed to be a sound engineer was in the basement of Johnny's house, and for some reason, the cops had raided that studio. Harvey didn't pick up.

Although I didn't have shit to do with their shit, Johnny started leaving messages threatening to have me deported if Harvey didn't pay him off. That communication led me to believe that Harvey was the real boss in their business. At that point, asking Harvey what was going on was a loaded question. Nevertheless, the gravity of this situation reassured me that it wouldn't be long before I had to go. I didn't come to America to get sucked into whatever shady, dangerous, or illegal shenanigans Harvey was involved in. Johnny's threats may have been empty, but he knew they would scare Harvey into action. Harvey's brain started cranking. I could see it. With all that effort, his brain made a tiny groove and spit out this whole big idea—*change careers*. It sounded like he was running from something too.

Harvey sobered up and went back to school, enrolling at UC Berkeley. We moved out of the house in the hills and into university family housing. Harvey wasn't going to school to get a degree; he just wanted to be a professional student with a family. Everything looked legitimate and normal on the outside. But inside our walls, I spiraled deeper into postpartum depression. I locked myself in Amelia's room and cried every night. Student housing was tight. I knew Harvey could hear me, but he never offered me any comfort. Instead, he'd knock on the door and tell me, "You don't need to lock your door. If there's a fire, I won't be able to save you."

Harvey would try to coax me out of the room by bribing

me with some of my favorite almond croissants from the local bakery, but I'd ask him to leave them on the kitchen counter. I knew what Harvey wanted. He didn't care about my mental state or show concern for Amelia. Harvey was kind only when he wanted sex.

My marriage was one big boot camp, and the training was helping me flow with random situations. Hopefully, I'd land on my feet as cats do, but if I didn't, I'd get back up.

I thought Harvey was slipping something into my food. Sometimes, I felt like I checked out, leaving my body behind. It wasn't a surprise when I ended up pregnant again. I went back to wondering who was in control because it didn't feel like it was me. Then again, no one pushed me into that situation, leaving no one to blame.

I couldn't say I landed precisely like a cat, but somehow, I was standing on both feet. I wanted to fly but seemed to fall flat on my face because I had only one wing. I needed two wings to fly. The moment I conceived, I knew this baby was the other wing. Without a shadow of a doubt, I believed that it was the sign that I would spread my wings to fly.

On my first prenatal visit, I went through a prescreening process, which involved some hard-core questions I had to think about. My replies, the truth, could change the planetary course of my life.

The social worker asked, "Were you ever sexually abused?"

Her patience told me that she cared, which made me feel I was in a safe space to answer her. I wanted to say yes, but I couldn't. I felt a massive boulder stuck in my throat, preventing the word from coming out. I stared at her kind face, hoping she'd understand that I was trying to say, "Yes, that shit happened to me!" She patiently waited until I could gather the courage to say the word and purge it from my system.

It took about an hour of us being in silence. She stayed with me the entire time, and following a big gasp for air, it finally came out. For the first time, I felt a sense of relief from the burden I thought I had to keep to myself. Ready or not, change was coming. I felt an immense sense of gratitude for the social worker asking me that question. She forged a connection between us, giving me the feeling that I was holding so much more inside me, and I needed to concede that the past was not who I was now. The new life growing inside me was courage, strength, and everything I needed to move on. Deep inside, this strained life with Harvey was devouring me. There was so much more, and the only way to find out what that entailed was to grow through it, to discover by way of experience.

After our initial meeting, the social worker checked on me to see how I was doing at home. She started coming over with a bag of groceries and then transitioned to taking the time to visit with me, but Harvey didn't like it. He thought the government was snooping around and spying on him. Becoming uncomfortable and furious, Harvey told the social worker to take her bag of groceries and shove it up her ass because he didn't need it. I don't think he noticed the bag wasn't for him, but it threatened him. He was uncomfortable when the social worker, or anyone, came over to talk to me. Harvey knew she was helping to remove the fear of growth and progress. Although I never told her about the mountain ridges, she reminded me that I was the little girl who dreamed big enough to travel beyond them.

Harvey started dropping me off at some yoga studio to learn breathing techniques. In certain moments I saw Harvey in a beautiful way and thought he really wasn't that bad. He could be better. He could stop cramming sex down my throat. If he stopped, I might have been inclined to offer him my potential, which I'm sure was there, somewhere buried deep in my gut, beneath the trauma. I didn't know precisely what I had to offer, but I knew I had something, and probably more than I knew. My experiences back home made me guarded. I wouldn't allow Harvey to just take my potential. I wouldn't permit him to rob me of the experience of giving it freely. I wasn't a flea market to be picked through. Harvey thought he was entitled. But where's the love in that? Love can't be bought or bargained for. Anyone deserving of love and intimacy should earn it. Truthfully, I hadn't worked to establish any intimacy either, which only contributed to that void between us. I learned that a relationship is work and a lot of the work focuses on oneself. Harvey certainly wasn't the right partner for me, but no person would ever be the right one until I had myself grounded in the right place. Only then could love come. I had a lot of shit to sort out and needed to work on myself and figure myself out. What did either of us expect, marrying a stranger because of desperation to get out of a shithole, or to have what we wanted?

The yoga class was full of pregnant women learning breathing techniques. Who would have thought that I needed to learn how to breathe? Isn't that the first thing we do when we're born? Yoga was good for me. I had so much in common with the other women that I felt at home with them in no time. I didn't know there was so much more to breathing than air flowing in and out. The mind controls the body, but who controls the mind? The breath. That's a load of control I was missing out on for not expanding my breathing capacity earlier.

◇◇◇◇◇◇◇◇◇◇◇

Amelia was two and a half years old, potty training, but still in diapers. Using her hands as a paintbrush, we played with watercolors. I was working on a poster-sized extreme close-up of my unborn child, and I couldn't figure out what to do with her head, so I left it open, dropping a big blob of paint right on her third eye as the final touch. I didn't know if she would be a boy or girl; I just wanted another healthy baby, so the three of us could fly away on our journey together. With every waking moment, life taught me that almost everything was happening as it should, and if not immediately, the lessons would come into play later.

On November 5, 1993, late in the afternoon, I felt the contractions. I placed little Amelia in the stroller and walked out the door. There wasn't going to be a home birth this time around. Harvey, returning home for his nap, met us on the sidewalk. I told him we were walking to the hospital. It was nearly ten blocks to Alta Bates Hospital in Berkeley, California. He shook his head and told me I was crazy to walk that far in my condition. He was right, but I was tired of him telling me what to do, so I kept walking—pushing Amelia in the stroller—and told him he could meet us there if he felt like it.

At the hospital, I told the front desk personnel that I was in labor and checking myself in. The nurse at the registration desk lowered her glasses and peered over the desk, sizing up a giant walking watermelon, then asked, "What makes you think you're in labor?"

"I'm having contractions," I told her. Then, nodding at Amelia, I added, "I've done this before, so I know what it's like. Are you going to give me a room?"

After some questions, she took Amelia and me to a room, and another nurse helped me get situated.

I thanked her. "This is my last labor, so I want to enjoy and make the best of it."

The nurse forced a smile. She seemed sleep deprived and too tired to care about anything. "Enjoy," she said as she left the room. She'd probably seen and heard it all before.

"Oh, wait!" I caught the door. "There's going to be a tall blond guy claiming to be my husband. Just ignore him if he barks at you."

She winked at me as the door shut.

A little while later, Amelia asked what we were doing. I explained, "There's going to be a new person that's going to come out of me today. It's going to be a great friend for you and me. And we're going to laugh together a lot."

Amelia smiled, displaying her tiny dimples. I reached in my bag and pulled out her coloring book and crayons to keep her preoccupied, but she didn't want to color. I patted the bed and asked, "Do you want to lay down with me?" Amelia reached for me. "Let's change your diaper first. It looks like it's sagging."

"You ready for baby, Mommy?"

"Yes, I'm scared, but ready because I have you with me, so it's going to be okay." After changing her diaper, I laid down. "Do you want to hold my hand while I close my eyes?" She nodded and sat by my side, holding my hand. "Don't go anywhere. I need my angel here with me."

A few minutes later, another nurse walked in and checked all my vitals. Then she put on a rubber glove, asked me to spread my legs, and stuck her hand in my vagina while asking how I was doing.

"I'm fine. But I just want to be clear, I've done this before. I don't want an episiotomy and would appreciate it if you didn't cut me without my permission."

She removed her hand from inside my vagina and hooked me up to a machine monitoring the baby's heart rate and intensity of the contractions.

"You're seven centimeters dilated," she told me.

I felt it and knew better than to scream for Advil, so I closed my eyes and took a deep yoga breath as if my life depended on it.

Deep breathing helped soothe every bone in my body and prevented me from screaming in pain. I was grateful that Harvey
wasn't there, especially at that moment because it was extraordi-
narily special. His presence would have undoubtedly sucked the
oxygen out of the room, flooding it with his predictable negative
vibe. Although I didn't know what possessed Harvey to send
me to prenatal yoga, I was grateful. I learned how to breathe
through life and breathe through the pain, and how essential
it all is. He could have sent me to learn how to fish, give him a
lap dance, or do something that would be for his pleasure. I had
gratitude for those decisions and believed that was his way of
caring about me—and his child.

"Oh shit! Here we go," I mumbled.

The pain was chewing every bone in my body, so I went
deeper in my breath for over twenty hours. The nurses and I
managed to keep Harvey out of the room throughout most of
my labor, but he hustled in now to ensure he got the placenta.
He'd learned about the benefits of the placenta and wanted to eat
the placenta of our second child. He believed the hospital would
profit from it, but instead, he wanted to reap the benefit.

Another nurse came in to take over the next shift, and I
immediately felt her vibrant energy. I knew right away she was
supposed to be at the birth with me. She said she had delivered
fifteen hundred babies, but she'd never seen one like this without
an epidural. Softly, I suggested to her that we should break the
sack. Within a half hour, a slimy baby came out—*another girl!* I
named her Asia.

Amelia was abruptly awakened by Asia's piercing scream.

"Wow, is that her?" She gazed lovingly and in awe at her
baby sister. She leaned in and touched her gently, like a delicate
porcelain doll.

I looked at my—*yes, my*—precious little girls with tremendous joy, and thought, *Now I have two girls to kick my ass.* Something about that highly inspired me—I knew I'd better get my shit together. And so—a mother was born.

4.

A Mother Crawling Out of Her Own Birth Canal

THE DAY AFTER A LONG LABOR, I SORTED AND DID laundry while Harvey was in the kitchen eating. The entire house smelled like me! Why? Harvey had cooked the placenta. Other than Harvey, I didn't know anyone who did that sort of thing. America wasn't a culture shock—*he* was a culture shock.

After crawling my way out of my own birth canal, feeling like a newborn, I took the first step to discover the new me. When I returned home, I had two kids. Overnight, I'd become a child-mother.

My village was a tiny little primitive box that I'd outgrown. But here I was with Harvey, in a fancy box made of plexiglass where he could watch my every move. I had to break out of this box too. When I realized that, a whole new creature emerged, and from that point, I was constantly in the process of transforming myself and came to embrace the holistic approach of rebirthing.

Harvey's concept of love manifested as an insatiable, consuming hunger to control me. His search for what he thought was love had collided with mine, and for a while I thought I loved him. But I was too young to know what love was. Before I could understand who Harvey truly was, I'd become a part of his journey. Harvey became a mode of transportation for me, a layover. I found myself simply riding along, but I quickly realized that we had different trajectories. I had such a hunger for life and love. I wouldn't stop learning and expanding my horizon. I needed to find that *Ahhh*—the thing I thought was missing. Once I discovered that what Harvey offered wasn't love, I could no longer shrink down to fit into his little box.

Amelia was the first experience I had where I wasn't thinking about or searching for love—*I was love*. I was innately exuding love from inside of me and being loved from inside of her—which helped me see that it is selfless. Because of my distorted perspective of Mama and her role in my life, I didn't see myself as a mother. I convinced myself that I didn't want to be like Mama, which was an intense awakening. I thought of how shocked I was to find that I was pregnant because I didn't believe my body was capable of it. The trauma I endured caused me to believe those things, and when I had Amelia, although it wasn't premeditated, my initial response was distant. Sadly, the damage from my childhood impacted my relationship with Amelia, but once I became aware, I refused to let it remain that way. I knew I needed to close the gap so Amelia could feel my love, and neither of my girls would go through what I went through. With Asia, I embraced it the moment I realized I was pregnant. My children played a crucial role in accelerating my growth and healing process as we raised one another.

Amelia's birth was the initial seismic event that catapulted me back into my body. Asia's birth completed the process. I now felt like I was truly inhabiting my body. The raw physical pain of being in labor for more than twenty hours swallowed all the other pain and forced me to acknowledge my body. Both deliveries were natural: no epidural, no painkillers, no support from Harvey. The excruciating sensations humbled me to surrender to the natural process and let the pain work with the body's inherent capacity to birth life. The grace of letting go cradled me as massive endorphins released. I felt my body undergo the intricate and miraculous process. I needed to be in the body to begin the process of waking up and healing from the inside out. To heal is to become conscious. To wake up is to be aware and witness what is happening in the mind, body, and heart. In this witnessing, that suffering ceased because I was simply the audience watching the drama onstage unfold. I merely observed the scenery before me, no longer identifying with or invested in it.

Being in the body afforded me the luxury of stepping back to experience life as it happened. It was my rebirth, and it was an ongoing transformative process that shifted the course of my life with grace, gratitude, and love. A process that guided me with ease and fulfillment, nudging me whenever I veered off course. I had more growing up to do; however, that was a great place to start.

Cradled against my breast was one-day-old Asia, and Amelia stayed safely nestled beside me. She even helped carry the laundry. It appeared insignificant, but time was valuable, and that was a way to spend time together. If someone didn't like how it looked, they could change how they looked at it. What people see and how they see things can reflect how they feel inside.

✧✧✧✧✧✧✧✧✧✧

After two beautiful girls and putting up with a lot of unnecessary shit, one would think I'd at least have a key to the mailbox.
But Harvey refused to give it to me, even when I asked. He
wanted me at his mercy even in this regard. I hadn't received
a single letter, and the last time I heard from any of my family
was the year prior. I knew that was odd, so I questioned whether
I had given them our new address when I wrote them. I told
Mama and my family that I was doing well—very well, how I
was excited to have another child, and that I would start school
soon. I didn't want them to worry about me, so I told them
all the good things. I was sure Mama would respond, asking
about Asia. When that didn't happen, I thought that either the
mailman accidentally delivered their letters to the neighbors, or
Harvey accidentally, and possibly on purpose, threw them out
with the junk mail. Harvey was paranoid. It wasn't just about
the mail. I still couldn't make or receive phone calls, especially
from the landline. He believed the line may have been tapped
and said, "You never know who's listening." There was more to
his story than I wanted to know. I didn't care about the phone. I
didn't know anyone anyway. If someone was listening, it was to
him. But I was desperate to hear from my family.

Curious to know if I had received any mail, I asked Harvey.

"Who would send you mail?" he replied, rubbing his hands
through his hair. "You wouldn't even get junk mail," he added
with a smirk. "People send letter bombs, and you never know
who might be sending *you* one. You certainly don't want an envelope exploding in your face. Or do you?"

"I'm missing letters from my family. Have you seen their
letters?"

"Letters! They can't afford postage, so they're not going to bother writing a letter."

During one of my wifely duties, cleaning, I found a pile of unopened mail, including a letter for me. When I picked up the white business-sized envelope, Harvey snatched it like a lightning bolt, but not before I noticed the letter was from the American Academy of Dramatic Arts. Harvey was shocked.

"Why would anybody from the American Academy of Dramatic Arts send *you* a letter? You? Not a chance," he said, releasing a heavy huff.

I shook my head, thinking, *This guy has no clue what I've been up to lately.* Two weeks prior, I saw an ad in the Sunday paper. Harvey routinely set aside the sections he had already read. When I saw the paper spread out on the dining table, an ad for the American Academy of Dramatic Arts caught my attention. They were holding auditions at the Saint Regis Hotel in downtown San Francisco. The ad listed famous actors such as Robert Redford and Anne Bancroft who attended the school. I didn't know much about dramatic arts, but something about the opportunity screamed adventure. I hadn't felt that excited in a while.

The day they were holding auditions, Harvey had plans and wouldn't be home. I placed Asia in my backpack carrier, Amelia in the stroller, and we caught the bus to downtown Berkeley where we took the train across the Bay Bridge. We got off a few blocks from the Saint Regis Hotel.

The audition was held in an intimidating yet grand ballroom. Other than a man conducting the interview, I was alone. The train ride knocked the girls out, and they were fast asleep while I did my monologue. I had gone to the Berkeley Library to read about monologues. The man seated in front of me gave me his full attention. "Whenever you're ready," he said.

I took a minute to steady my breath before delivering a

monologue about pregnancy from the novel *Heartburn* by Nora Ephron. I resonated with the piece so profoundly that it became a reprieve from my experience. Delivering the monologue was an outlet.

During the monologue, the empty ballroom began hosting an audience.

When I finished, the man asked me to do a cold read.

"Please explain what a cold reading is?" I asked politely.

He handed me a three-page script and explained that he wanted me to read this piece of text that I'd never seen before. After a few deep breaths, I went for it. He didn't offer any feedback when I finished. Regardless of the results, I felt a great sense of accomplishment. I'd done what I wanted, which made me feel fucking amazing!

"Thank you," the man said. I thanked him in return with so much excitement that it nearly caused me to twirl him around and jump on him. But instead, I got my girls bundled up in the stroller, floated out of the ballroom and down the streets of San Francisco back to the train station. The floating thing stayed with me for a while.

Closer to home, we stopped at some kiddie park where Amelia got on the slides while I placed Asia softly in a baby swing. I met this hippie girl, Alex, who was babysitting for a family in the neighborhood, and we hit it off. She told me she liked that I was Filipino because she collected authentic Filipino recipes. She could have gone to the library, but she wanted recipes handed down from generations. I told her my grandmother once showed me how to make boiled egg and okra so perfectly slimy and soft that it slides down your throat. Alex gave me her phone number and invited me to come over to her place so she could make us a gourmet dinner. Some hippie guy approached us, and when Alex turned around, they started making out. I found it refreshing to see two shameless people just going at it. When I said goodbye, Alex managed a quick introduction and goodbye at the same time. Then, as the stroller hit the sidewalk, she shouted, "Call me!"

When Harvey tore open the letter from the American Academy of Dramatic Arts, the first thing he saw was "Congratulations!" He looked like his heart sank. It was an acceptance letter offering a full scholarship. I didn't plan on attending; I just wanted the experience of auditioning. Some people are blind when it comes to other people's potential. And just because you can't see it doesn't mean it's nonexistent.

Before he could hit me with a barrage of questions, I insisted, "Oh, honey, that's some junk mail."

Harvey sensed a sudden change in the weather forecast. But he played it cool because he didn't think I was going anywhere. Why would I? He was confident that I could never leave him. "Where would she go?" he'd say to himself. "She doesn't know anyone. She doesn't even have any money." But Harvey didn't know I had just met that hippie girl, and she seemed alright. Finally, I might have a new friend.

I looked at Harvey and said to myself, *I'm from the jungle, honey, dear. I can swing from vine to vine. I might fall flat on my face, but I'll get my ass up.* My once bankrupt ego was riding the inflation. I needed to get myself all pumped up.

5.

Divine Delivers on Time

WHAT SHOULD I PACK IF I WERE TRAVELING LIGHT and could take only four things with me? Where would I go? I didn't know. But I started a new journey in May of 1994 that would only take a hundred steps to begin. Ninety-nine of those steps were a piece of cake. The first step was the one I had to worry about. I didn't need to overthink it, or I'd think my way out of it. First, I needed to sort out the stuff I needed to take. Glancing around the apartment made my choices easy. Amelia, Asia, a backpack for their clothes, and the stroller. What else? I didn't own anything, so at least there was nothing I'd miss.

When I started placing the girl's clothing in the backpack, I still didn't know anything about America, and the available options, but oddly, I was calm. I wasn't going to explore something bigger or someone better over a mountain ridge. This time I was searching for Deja. I didn't love Harvey. I probably never did. I certainly never felt for him even a fraction of what I had felt for Taylor, so something was missing, or wrong. I couldn't settle.

I got the girls together and decided to take them for a walk to clear my head. I headed to the park, hoping to see my new and only friend Alex, but when I arrived at the park, it was empty—and no sight of Alex either. The girls and I had the whole park to ourselves.

I put Amelia in a swing and pushed her, asking, "Do you want more?"

With so much excitement, she'd scream, "Yes!"

I'd say, "Here you go!" and push her even higher, with Asia watching from the baby swing next to her.

We had nothing but each other, and we were happy. The girls and I continued playing for a couple of hours, but no one else came. I began to understand that this was America; you don't expect to randomly run into people like I did in the village. If I wanted to see people, I'd have to call them and make an appointment. We left the park and went home, and I saw the mailman's truck parked on the sidewalk. The mailman was at the entrance of the apartment building dispersing mail in the mailboxes. I'd never met him before or even seen him.

I walked up to him and asked, "Is there any mail for me? I'll take junk mail."

The mailman asked for my name. I told him, and he began sifting through a pile of mail.

"Here you go," he said, handing me an envelope.

"Just one mail?" I asked, and he nodded. "I'll take it."

It had my name on it, but I couldn't tell from the outside of the envelope who sent it, so I anxiously ripped the letter open only to find there was nothing to read, but there was a green plastic card with my picture on it. My green card! Good gracious, I completely forgot about it. I threw myself at the old mailman, wrapping my arms around him, and nearly gave him a heart attack.

The following day, I packed the girls in the stroller and finished filling the backpack with their clothes. Harvey was sitting on the sofa across from the door. I thought it would be rude not to say anything. He was reading or pretending to study for an exam, oblivious that I was walking out the door. Since I wasn't carrying a suitcase, maybe he thought I was going to the laundromat or running some errand.

I paused before the door shut behind me, backed up a little, and said rather calmly, "Honey, I'm leaving. I want the children, and I would leave them with you if I thought they would be okay, but I think they're better off with me." Harvey barely looked up, but I knew I had his attention and needed to be delicate because he was six foot three and could easily stop me. "I just want my children," I restated. "Oh, don't worry, I'm not leaving you for another man. I'm leaving you for me."

He didn't reply right away, but judging from the look on Harvey's face, he heard every word, so I gave him a moment to respond.

"I warned you before. If you leave me, you'll be selling yourself *and* those girls on the street! Then you'll be crawling back to me soon enough!"

Harvey knew he was getting a great deal, which is why he didn't bother to fight about it. *Okay, enough of this nonsense. I can't waste my precious energy on this kind of shit.* The important thing was to walk out the door.

Then I remembered one more thing. "Oh, honey, happy anniversary!"

It was our fourth anniversary. What can I say? My timing was impeccable. I left my diamond ring on the table. I could have sold it and used the money, but the value in giving it back to Harvey was greater.

I had less than a hundred dollars and two children, but all I needed was fresh air. If I had that, I had an abundance. I was like my father. As a young man, he'd fled the farm where he worked, practically as a slave, and went to town. He wore two sets of clothing and had nothing in his hands when he left.

That first step marked the beginning of a new journey. Everything before that first step was crawling.

The great thing about having nothing is that I had nothing to lose. But I had the opportunity to develop resilience. Resilience is like the Incredible Hulk. Every time he gets hit, it makes him stronger and angrier. Only, I didn't get angry. Instead, I chose to get stronger and wiser. Every setback gave me more hope and a stronger conviction, and helped me adapt in situations and to act accordingly moving forward. Rather than dwell on what wasn't working, I've learned to focus on what is working.

The girls and I had walked in and out of that apartment door hundreds of times, but that last time, everything was different. First, I pushed the stroller to the sidewalk just as the fresh ocean breeze swept across my face. Then I took off and ran as fast as I could for three blocks—constantly checking behind me in case *someone* decided to chase after us. But, no Harvey. He was pretty confident I'd be selling my body once I hit the streets and would crawl back to him. The worst part was that he showed me he didn't care about his children. His little girls meant nothing to him, but they were everything to me. Convinced that he wasn't coming after me, I stopped running to catch my breath and gather my thoughts.

I wasn't worried about not having anywhere to go. I was amused and astonished that I left with nothing but my daughters. As long as Amelia and Asia saw my face, they didn't seem to care. One day I would explain what happened after I figured it all out, so I focused on the long day ahead of us. I couldn't think about tomorrow. I focused on one moment at a time.

When I turned the corner, I spotted a pay phone and dug some quarters out of my pocket that I had left from doing the laundry. I called Alex. She told me she was home and taking the rest of the day off to mend her broken heart. I asked if it was okay if we stopped by. Although I wasn't brokenhearted, I told her I had left my husband, piquing her curiosity.

"You did?" she asked.

She told me she had broken up with that hippie guy she made out with at the park, but she sounded thrilled to have company. She said she would have picked us up, but her car broke down.

"No worries. We'll take the bus."

Alex told me which buses to take to get to her place. I let her know I wasn't familiar with the route, but we'd get there at some point.

While waiting at the bus stop for the second bus ride, I noticed a huge free-standing building right across the street. I watched one mother carrying her two children come out and another mother carrying a child go in. Something told me I should go in to check it out. I came to find that it was the welfare office. There were no lines, so I went straight to the counter.

The clerk said, "How can I help you?"

"I don't know," I replied, trying to figure out what to ask.

Since it wasn't busy, I had time to tell her my story. After fifteen minutes, I spoke with a caseworker who got all the paperwork together and had me sign a few things and show her my green card. When the caseworker told me I was all set, she said I should receive a check every month for $650 plus food stamps and some food vouchers, but I needed to get back to her with my address. We went all over town looking for an apartment.

My budget was $500 to $650 a month, and every place I went turned me down on the spot. Since it was getting late, and the girls were tired of being cooped up in the stroller, we headed to Alex's place.

Alex was happy to see us, and she was kind enough to make us dinner. After that, she pulled out her sofa bed for us to sleep on in her living room and then went out on a date with a new guy. Later that night, she came home with someone. In less than a minute, I heard the headboard banging against the wall. I rolled over and went back to my sleep.

The next day, I left early with the girls and walked all over town again, apartment hunting. They all turned me down right on the spot. I was about to give up for the day when I found a perfect studio for $500. I told the owner, "There's absolutely no reason why you won't give me this place. I'll have my caseworker send you the rent directly, so you don't have to worry about me missing the rent, unless you discriminate against children. That would be the only reason why you wouldn't rent me this place." I asked to use her telephone to call my caseworker and give her my new address. Afterward, she handed me the lease agreement to sign. We carried everything we owned, so we were able to move in on the spot. The beauty of traveling light. For the first time, we had a place of our own.

◇◇◇◇◇◇◇◇◇◇◇◇

Although Harvey told Mama and Papa that he would send me to college, going was my responsibility, so I enrolled at Laney College in the fall of 1994. Laney was a community college in Oakland, California, where I majored in film and television. A combination of grants, scholarships, and childcare assistance made it possible for me to go. The best part was that as a student, I had access to Laney's studio, and studio time was something I looked forward to. I discovered early on that I felt at home on set.

◇◇◇◇◇◇◇◇◇◇

Sometimes, crossing the muddy rice paddy, I'd look at the horizon and see things in frames. Growing up, my sister, some of our friends, and I would get together and go out toward the mountains to the coconut groves and get the baby coconuts to eat. We would get a ton of coconut meat by scooping it out into a bucket. We had a massive coconut picnic amid coconut groves throwing some milk in the bucket and eating it with biscuits—it was so good!

Then the dirt path the farmers made got flooded when the irrigation system broke, but that didn't deter us. Sometimes, we'd have to take a giant leap to get across the dirt path, and I'd tell everyone when to jump. We had a cheap camera with 110 film cartridges and twenty-four exposures. There was one moment when everyone jumped, trying not to land in the muddy water, and I snapped a picture. I loved capturing a moment while everyone was in action. That shot stuck with me.

When I went to school, the welfare office told me that I had to take a class that would teach me a trade. Since I was in film class, they agreed to count that as a trade, as long as I was in school. I chose film because it was instinctive. Studying film provided another opportunity to explore life without someone telling me what to do, and I loved that. I didn't know where it would take me, but I finally found something that I felt passionate about.

With filmmaking, I directed, produced, and got it done the way I wanted. I sank my teeth into the whole creative process, and I saw it was a collaborative effort with many facets. I studied so I could command as a director. But after I learned as much as I had, I didn't want to do it alone anymore. I wanted to work with a great team, and I realized an incredible film starts with a great script. Not mediocre—great. I studied screenwriting for the following three years. During the first year, I struggled to write a ten-page screenplay in a single day. Of course, everyone wanted their scenes to be perfect, but the struggle I saw within me was understanding and recognizing the conceptual and intuitive side of my brain and what that looked like on the page. They fired up without my calling them into command. It was as though I understood both sides of my brain. To have both fired up at the right time was overwhelming at first until I got the hang of it. Mastery of the duo is crucial to my writing process in taking commands of this craft.

Film required me to understand the craft, have a vision, know how to execute that vision, and connect with life to get the vision. I had such a passion for storytelling and wanted to share it with the world.

On set, I had loads of fun collaborating with different personality types. I had to take command technically and especially creatively, which got my juices going. That was the best thing I learned from that institution. It forced me to search within and identify what it was about storytelling that I was passionate about. Filmmaking gave me the freedom to explore creativity and bring together different elements to execute a vision with a unique, authentic voice. It was what I did when I came to America. I held a childhood vision of my innate creativity being my career, and it had to be executed. It had to manifest. My love for filmmaking came from a deep resonance that life is one big fucking play and filmmaking was the ultimate medium to execute that play. And to create reality infused with feelings, thoughts, words, actions, and the fattest attitude one can muster that's born out of passion and inspiration—that was empowering. It reinforced that *I was finally in charge*. I was the play, the fucking star, the villain, and the director. I wanted a play that reflected the absurdity of life. That no matter how life seemed to hit bottom, it's nothing serious. That there is grace. That I have a choice between tragedy or comedy. I could make that play however I wanted! Did I want it to feel epic? Did I care how it might affect others? Maybe I didn't. Or perhaps I wanted to blow people's minds if I put my heart and soul into it. I had to let go and allow myself to fucking play! I could wear all the different hats. When I allowed myself to sink into that mindset, I gave myself permission to have fun in the process. Then, I started to remember who I was and who I am.

Ever since I could remember, I've experienced lucid dreaming. I attribute this trait to my grandfather. Vibrant colors with three-dimensional sounds bombard me night and day. And the only way for me to make peace with them is to recreate them. It's my way of acknowledging their much-welcomed intrusion into my disarrayed psyche. The process satisfies my deep hunger for creativity and transmuted my insatiable bloody sexual appetite into a level of divine intercourse.

I had five classes in film and TV, and three of them were taught by the same teacher. One class was on the history of film and television, my least favorite class. In that class, my brain would automatically check out on me. One day, I was on the bus to Laney, and the bus stopped across the street from Claremont Club & Spa, and a brilliant idea hit me. I got off the bus and walked over to the hotel lobby with excitement. A moment later, I was in the spa's steam room naked while my body was drinking the steam. I should have been in Mr. Parson's history class, but with school and the girls, I needed to steal a little time to nurture and nourish my mind, body, and soul. From that perspective, I thought it would put me in a better mindset to do great things. Only that wasn't the first time I played hooky during his class period. I loved the next class, which was production. I never skipped that one. Production took place in the studio, and the projects were hands on with cameras, lighting, and sound equipment. When I discovered that being in front of and behind the camera felt natural, I made sure to be on time for the studio roll call. But that day, I enjoyed having the whole spa to myself!

I missed only Mr. Parson's class, and I was never late to the studio. But Mr. Parson missed me, and he called me into his office to tell me how much. I was hoping to warm up the chair with my perfectly steamed-up ass, but he didn't give me a chance to sit down. Although I didn't go to every one of his classes, I stayed on top of my work. But that didn't matter—I'd given him an opportunity to tell me what he thought, and he read me the riot act. "You are *never* going to make it in this industry because you're a minority, and to top it off, *a woman*," he said.

That wasn't quite what I was expecting, so I was shocked at the outburst of negative and disparaging comments. However, it was exactly what I needed. Mr. Parson was right. But I heard something else reverberating at the other end of the tunnel. The reason I wouldn't make it was precisely the same reason I would. I had to turn things to work to my advantage. Perspective. All I could say to him was "Thank you, Mr. Parson. Thank you."

He echoed the same underlying sentiment as Harvey.

◇◇◇◇◇◇◇◇◇◇◇◇

My landlady refused to return my calls about fixing the refrigerator. I didn't know what was wrong with it, but it was dead. There was no hot water, and the vintage furnace leaked toxic fumes. After about two weeks of calling her with no response, I decided I'd get her attention another way.

I was cleaning the apartment with Asia giggling in a carrier on my back when there was a loud pounding on the door. I answered to find the landlady standing in front of me, arms folded beneath her breast, wearing an overly exaggerated disgruntled expression as she demanded the rent. After weeks of calling about the problems in my apartment to no avail, I said, "I'm not paying any rent until you fix things around here."

Speaking to me as if I was a stupid, immigrant, single mother leaching off welfare, she threatened to evict us. When I signed the lease, I had offered to have my caseworker wire my landlord the rent directly, but she never took me up on that offer— something I'm sure she regretted at this moment.

"You can try to evict me, but I'm not paying any rent until you fix things. And if that's what you want to do, it's going to cost you ten times more to try to evict me than if you would just fix this stuff."

She didn't like that I had the guts to speak up.

While I was having issues with my landlady, a woman who lived in the complex, Devon, came over, eager to help. She knew Harvey from some previous business dealings, though he never mentioned her before. Devon told me she was a single mom and understood exactly what I was going through. I was moved and appreciated the help. I didn't want to ask anyone because I was afraid they would take advantage of me, and I didn't know who to go to anyway.

I took Devon up on her offer to help me find another place. We found one close to UC Berkeley's campus. It was a cute cottage behind the main house with a separate yard in a good neighborhood. It was within walking distance of everything, but it needed a lot of work. The owner agreed to keep the rent at

$500 since I agreed to fix it up. I had no problem putting in the labor. With Devon's help, I renovated the bathroom, painted the entire place, did some landscaping, bought a new refrigerator. Devon even paid for the materials. Once done, the place looked fantastic.

We didn't have a lot of furniture, but we didn't need a lot. There was a small couch in the living room, but I did want to get the girls a nice set of wooden bunk beds. Only it was too costly. So I studied the construction of it at the store. Berkeley had a great tool library; I could borrow everything except a bulldozer. Inspired, I went to Home Depot, bought some wood materials, and in five days, I'd made and varnished bunk beds for Amelia and Asia. They looked better than the ones in the store, and they didn't require palm leaves like the bed I had growing up. I was proud of their custom-made bunk beds, which was the most valuable thing we owned.

As soon as the girls and I were getting settled, Devon revealed that not only did she know Harvey, but she had dated him too. Then she told me the real reason she helped me.

"I want you to work for me," she stated, but it wasn't a question.

I asked, "Doing what?"

"Sales."

"Sales? I don't have experience selling. And what exactly are we selling?"

She didn't want to say unless I agreed to work for her. Given her hesitation, I didn't want to hear it either. I gathered it was something of an illegal nature—especially if Harvey was involved. Maybe he sent her to target me so they could use me in some scheme.

I told her, "Thank you very much for all your help, but no, thank you. We are okay. More than okay."

I didn't feel like I owed her a penny, not one bit, because that was not a condition of her helping us, and she had misrepresented who she was and her intent. It was sufficient to say thank you and usher her ass out the door.

◇◇◇◇◇◇◇◇◇◇◇◇

Tilden Park in Berkeley was packed that summer. I took the girls one day to spend time with their mama, get some fresh air, and enjoy the merry-go-round. We had some snacks and a lot of laughter that afternoon. It was always a joy to have time to play with my girls.

Behind the concession stand was Drake. He reminded me of a soccer superstar I had a crush on in high school, a boy who seemed to have everything going for him. He was cute, smart, and rich. Most of the kids, including me, walked to school wearing holey flip-flops. Those who were a little better off took a cab. A rare few, like the soccer kids, got dropped off in a four-wheel drive, which was equivalent to being chauffeured in a Bentley.

Drake was manning the carousel. Though I noticed him, initially I didn't think much of him. When the girls and I went for the second round of the stiff horse ride, Drake gave me this ride-all-day smile. It landed. He was six foot one and the clean-cut heartthrob type, with short dirty blond hair and baggy, loose-fitting jeans to compensate for his slightly boney physique—and to hide his undefined pectoral region, which I came to learn he was self-conscious about. Drake was a sweetheart, but that felt like a distraction that cloaked a monster itching to claim its prey. I thought he was younger than me, never had a girlfriend before, and certainly never heard of diapers. I walked away, dismissing his flirtation, asserting I didn't have time for him. Drake was persistent, seeming to like children, *my children.* For a moment, something didn't feel right, and I was afraid, but I was quick to dismiss it as PTSD. My thoughts raced back to my uncles and my cousin, which made me sick. But I didn't want to judge this stranger, Drake, by my experiences. That was then—I was over the mountain ridge now. After a couple of rounds on the carousel, he came over and asked if he could get my number. Still reluctant, I gave it to him because I didn't know many people, and I noticed how quickly he took to my girls. It was nice to see someone else making them laugh, especially since Harvey wasn't around, and when we had lived with him, they were invisible to him.

The following day, Drake called asking me to go out with him.

I said, "Thank you, but, no, I come with a big package."

"I know, and that's cool. Can I hang out with you *and* the kids?"

I was impressed. Drake exceeded my limited expectation of the untouchable schoolboy crush. But I was right about him being younger; he was, by a month, and he had never had a girlfriend. He told me that he lived with his friends. He was persistent, and I didn't know what to say, but I liked that, and him, so I agreed.

Dating was a strange concept to me. It was something you did as a teenager. I skipped that period and went straight to marriage. Clearly, that didn't work out, so I didn't have a clue as to what dating meant.

Drake arrived at my door the day of our date with his mother. *What the fuck?* I thought. Either she was there to screen me or she was his chauffeur. Settling on the latter, I nicknamed her Bentley. Her real name was Cathy, and everything about her screamed top of the line. She was an accountant and probably studying me based on my subtle facial twitches to see if my psyche was fragile. But I didn't feel outwardly judged. She was too sophisticated for that. She was the type to make me feel warm and welcomed first, and I did, but I also felt like she was analyzing me. Cathy had probably worked out a strategy on how she would talk Drake out of his romantic notions with an immigrant single mother of two. I didn't think I was what she had planned for her golden boy. I got it. I was on the same page with her and one step ahead. I was used to being analyzed and people not thinking I was good enough.

◇◇◇◇◇◇◇◇◇◇◇◇

The landlord told me he was increasing the rent, and I was sick. When I rented the place it was a dump. Now that it was all fixed up, he wanted it back because he could rent it for more.

I was getting pretty good at catching people trying to take advantage of me, so I told him, "What? After all that work I put in? I'm not paying more rent. You'll have to take me to court for that."

He was scared to take me to court because it would cost him much more than my rent, while it wouldn't cost me anything. Welfare provided special legal benefits. But this landlord decided to get me another way by calling Child Protective Services on me. Why? Parental negligence for not having vaccinated my girls.

Two women came knocking on my door unannounced. I was kind and welcomed them in. One of them told me who they worked for and then asked if I knew what they were there for. It took only a split second to figure out who was behind the call. But these two women couldn't have picked a better time to drop in on me. It was a chill afternoon; our place was super clean and I was in the middle of making a healthy beet salad. We could afford fresh produce only because we went to the farmers market when the vendors started packing up at the end of the day, and they pretty much gave away whatever leftovers they had. We usually ended up with plenty of fresh fruits and vegetables to last us the week. They went to the kitchen and opened the refrigerator, checking to see if anything was in it. I didn't know what they were looking for, but they were not finding any of it in my place. My girls had just woken up from their naps, and both of them, with shaved heads, climbed into my lap, half asleep and oblivious to the two strange women in the room.

One of the women spoke up and asked, "Why did you shave their heads?"

"Their hair gets tangled, and when it comes back, it's thicker," I said with conviction, rubbing the top of my girls' heads.

"Do you smoke or drink?"

"No. And no. Do you see a can of beer? Or a cigarette butt anywhere?"

Then they brought up the issue of vaccination—just another thing that people immediately seize upon to think of me as stupid. Most everybody else vaccinates their children, so if I don't, then that must make me stupid. The "stupid" part didn't bother me; rather it was the fact that they were there to take my children because they implied I was a negligent parent. Amelia had the first vaccines of diphtheria, polio, and tetanus and had a bad reaction, so I opted not to give any further inoculation. I got a book and read about other medical perspectives, and I stuck with that decision. I didn't understand the seriousness of the repercussions until the women showed up and tried to take my babies.

I had less than a dozen books on my shelf. *Zen Mind, Beginner's Mind* by Shunryu Suzuki, *The Power of Positive Thinking* by Norman Vincent Peale, and the rest were books on the pros and cons of vaccinations. Some were written by doctors who were parents themselves and had chosen not to vaccinate their children. Since reading those books, I could articulately speak about vaccinations and defend my decisions. I pulled those points of reference from the shelf, and, pissed, dropped them in front of the women. I said, "I chose not to vaccinate my children with an informed decision."

I didn't mind their intrusion. But nobody can just roll into my place and think they have any right to take my children.

Then, one of the women said, "The thing is, you can't take your children to school because if they are not vaccinated, no school will take them."

"That's not true. Amelia's in school. Maybe not at the moment, but she is enrolled in public pre-K. There's a release form that's a kind of waiver for parents who choose not to vaccinate their kids. I always ask for that form because no one knows about it unless it's requested. Do you know about the waiver?" Both shook their heads. They didn't know that it existed. "Well, that information is not out there unless you search for it. The point for me is not about vaccination, but about whether you choose vaccination or not, make an informed decision. It's personal. It's worked for us."

They could see my children looked healthy. They had nothing on me. And they couldn't find evidence to support their recommended case against me by my landlord. The women apologized for their intrusion and left graciously.

As soon as they left, I looked at the girls, sitting contently and well rested on the couch. My face lit up as I thought, *What angels I've been blessed with.*

◇◇◇◇◇◇◇◇◇◇◇

I desperately needed to unplug from the matrix. Something about society was sucky—plagued with greed and fear. A mentality of lack was driving people. Although there was plenty, they still felt it was not enough. That is where suffering derived. I felt there was an innate call to dissolve into Mother Nature's lap and reset—that couldn't wait. There I wouldn't need anything because I never had anything to need. I survived as a minimalist, or without anything other than love. Life is not easy, but it is simple.

I told Drake, whom I had been seeing since that first date, we were leaving but didn't think he took me seriously. I sold everything we had, then packed up our clothing and left. We didn't have a lot to sell, but I got three offers for the bunk beds. I sold it to a grandmother who had sole custody of her two grandchildren because the dad was a deadbeat, and the mom was in jail. She wasn't the highest bidder, but I thought she needed it the most. I'd heard about the Rocky Mountains. It sounded like Mother Nature's lap and just the place to restore my spirit. I saved up a thousand dollars and bought three plane tickets to Denver, Colorado, with a student credit card. I was trying to establish credit, and at least that was a start.

While in flight, as the aircraft ascended higher in altitude, I watched Berkeley become smaller until it was gone. It felt good not to be bogged down by the future or the past because my brain wanted nothing to do with it. It was exhausting. I wanted to enjoy the present. I knew that sounded irresponsible, but I believed it to be quite the opposite. I was looking forward to the Rocky Mountains for some massive rejuvenation, and I needed to continue my healing journey. I hadn't written to my family in the Philippines for a few years, and I needed to reconnect, but if they knew what I was doing, they would freak out. They like to worry, which is why I went ahead and did my thing. My mind was wrapped up in getting somewhere, and I didn't know what to say to my family. "How are you"? "We're homeless"? Although not hearing from me was probably freaking them out just as much. But I had to keep moving. I had an overwhelming need to disconnect and to connect in another capacity. As a little girl, I instinctively resorted to Mother Nature as my source of renewal and self-discovery. While I hadn't embraced it yet, I was learning to love myself, and all along I was reflecting the deeper source of true love—the liberating insight that it all begins with loving oneself came from the silent whisper of nature. When I was in solitude, my awareness grew, which was a crucial part of my process and something I didn't think I could explain to anyone. The only thing I needed to do was allow myself to let go of the mental chatter and quiet my mind. I had the perfect companions in Amelia and Asia. My girls understood me best.

6.

Be Still and Know That I Am
God Watching Over You

W E LANDED IN DENVER, COLORADO. I WAS FILLED
with excitement to begin this part of my journey. I was
having my period and it was uncomfortable for me to
move, but I managed. Most people have someone meet them at
the airport, but this case was extraordinary. Though no person
was waiting for us—God was there. He wanted me to feel Him,
in form or without form. He showed me that even if you don't
think anyone picked you up, He is there with you. *Remember to
whom you are connected*, I thought. That was a moment of arrival
when I did what I was supposed to do. I felt God say to me, "Be
still and know that I am God."

We didn't know where we would sleep that night because I
hadn't made any arrangements: no hostel, no friend, just nature—
and God is nature. I felt everything would work out, though I

didn't know how. The only thing I knew for sure was that we were going to Boulder, only I didn't know how to get there from the airport. Even with two young girls, there was no sense worrying about it. Worrying wouldn't solve the issue. Worrying is praying for something I don't want. So why worry. Great things were happening. I had Amelia by my side, Asia in her carrier, a backpack for their clothes, and a small tent. That was everything we needed.

First things first, we sat on a bench—quiet and still, ignoring the movements around us. Just being there, taking in the scenery and fresh air, was a vacation. Less of everything seemed like more of the good things, like resting on the branch of a mango tree. Since we weren't in a hurry and no one was waiting for us, I continued to sit in a relaxed meditative state until I got the urge to move.

After her moment of stillness had passed, four-year-old Amelia calmly asked, "Mommy, what are we going to do next?"

"I don't know, sweetie. But do you see that woman standing over there in the blue sweater?" I asked, nodding in the woman's direction a few feet away.

"Yes."

"Why don't you ask her what time it is?"

Amelia skipped over to her without a care in the world while I watched.

It turned out that the woman was waiting for the bus bound for Boulder too. She told me it was a beautiful hour-and-a-half ride. I thought it might be good to go in the same direction with someone who knew where they were going. The woman told me about this great camping place called Nederland, southwest of Boulder. The way she described it sounded exactly like the place calling me.

We made it to Boulder before sunset. Again, we sat quietly

by a street corner and took in the surroundings. I don't know why, but again, I wasn't going to move until I felt the urge, but I couldn't take too long; the girls were getting restless, and I knew we needed to get some food, then find a place to sleep.

An older man walked by, and I asked, "Excuse me, is there a hostel close by?"

"Sure is. There's one about five blocks away," the man said, pointing north.

Just then, we walked past a bicycle store that was about to close for the day. But outside was a display for a collapsible blue-and-yellow double buggy with three big wheels on sale for 75 percent off the original price. I couldn't pass up that deal. It was perfect for us. The girls could ride in it and sleep when we had to walk far, and I could run with that buggy, the same way I ran when I thought Harvey might have been chasing behind us.

We made it to the hostel and settled in for the night. The following morning, after taking full advantage of the hostel's complimentary breakfast of boiled eggs and toast, we headed out to catch the bus to Nederland. We were the only three passengers.

About twenty minutes into the ride, Amelia asked, with wide eyes full of curiosity, "Why aren't we with Daddy?"

I wanted to answer her with the truth. She deserved that much, especially since she was inquisitive enough to ask. She knew she had a daddy, and she also was aware that we had been on our own for a long time. Regardless, she needed to know the reason that she no longer saw him. We didn't talk about him. But since it crossed her mind, I had to address it in the most efficient manner so she wouldn't think about it again. It wasn't worth peeling back the layers of negativity and all the intricate details; that was history. She was too young, and the whole conversation wasn't a conversation for a child. The bottom line was that he wasn't interested in being a part of their lives.

I kept it simple and replied to her question as though she were my equal. "Because we are better off without him."

She didn't say or ask anything more. Amelia leaned her head against me and looked out the window.

Truthfully, I rarely thought about Harvey. I needed to focus on what was in front of me, the two beautiful girls in my arms. We weren't hiding from him. He could find us if he wanted to, but he didn't. Amelia's question caused me to reflect. It was more than just a momentary curiosity. There was a particular tone to the way she asked, pushing her words to reverberate in my bones. It was as if she'd been thinking about it all that time—all those years. It was troubling and disheartening that Amelia had that thought circulating in her four-year-old brain. She'd been chewing on and digesting why her father wasn't present in her life. I didn't think that he was present in his own life. I lived with him under the same roof for four years exactly up until that day we walked out, but he wasn't around much, and if he was, he wasn't present and available. He'd slip off into another room somewhere. And going to the park with the girls was out of the question. He always looked busy. I'm sure it never occurred to my daughter that I was trying my hardest to create distance from that man to have my own space, so that I could breathe.

We were sitting in the last seat of the bus when the driver yelled, "Where are you going?"

"We're going to this campsite in Nederland," I replied.

"I'm not going that far. The last stop is about seven miles from that campsite."

"Okay, what can you do?" We'd have to walk seven miles. Simple as that.

There was a tourist information booth next to the bus stop. I went over to ask for a map, but the lady behind the counter was on the phone. She motioned for me to hold on. And since I didn't know what direction to head, I patiently waited until she got off the phone. As soon as she hung up, and before I could say anything, she announced, "Someone's coming to drive you to the campsite—Ms. Margaret. She'll talk a bit, but they don't get any sweeter."

I didn't know who told her to arrange the ride for us, but I was grateful for the kindness. I take it when it comes, and it came when I needed it. And sure enough, three minutes later, the sweetest old lady pulled up to the curb. With sun-kissed, silver-gray hair in a long perfect braid down the middle of her back and the most peaceful smile, Ms. Margaret leaned over to the passenger side of her station wagon and pushed the door open.

"It's our ride," I told the girls cheerfully.

"Do you have everything you need?" she asked.

"Yes, we do," I said, eyeing my girls while Amelia wrapped her arms around my leg. "We have each other," I added, kissing the top of Asia's head as I gently scooted Amelia into the back seat.

Ms. Margaret told us it would be a beautiful ride and advised Amelia, "Try not to miss anything. You might see a moose or two. And if you're lucky, maybe one with its babies like your mama and you two girls."

Ms. Margaret made small talk, and I mostly listened. She told us about the wildlife and the area. I felt my excitement rising as I got closer to home—nature! Like the girls, I took in the view and started connecting with Mother Nature. The scent of the lush green pine trees infused with the fresh air made the magnificent seven-mile drive up the snaking road even more majestic. The weather couldn't have been more perfect for camping, although nobody seemed to be at the campsite other than us.

Ms. Margaret asked, "Do you need anything? It doesn't look like you've got much?"

"We'll be okay," I reassured her.

"When should I come back to pick you up?"

"I'm not sure," I told her. I hadn't fully connected with Mother Nature yet, and we weren't leaving until I had.

"If you need something, I can bring it back when I come," she said, sounding like the most loving grandmother.

"We should be okay. We have some dry food to eat for now, but I don't know how long we're going to stay. I guess until the food runs out," I replied with a bit of laughter. "Thank you, kindly."

Ms. Margaret said she'd come back to check on us in a few days. Then she pulled off.

While carrying Asia on my back, Amelia and I built the tent together. Then we went for a run around the meadows because they were waiting for us. Pure joy! And that had everything to do with being in nature. My lungs were so happy to breathe, and my soul was bathing in the sweet caress of Mother Nature. Such an extraordinary moment. I felt so lucky to be alive. I was so in the moment savoring nature's delicious abundance while nourishing every fiber of my being, I wasn't hungry.

As nightfall began, I got the girls settled under the evening sky with mini cinnamon rice cakes and almond butter next to a crackling bonfire we made from the pine cones and wood we collected. Soon after, the little ones were ready for bed. I tucked them in the tent, and they fell fast asleep. The amber, burning log enamored me. I didn't realize how much I missed my home under the sky.

Suddenly, I felt someone tapping my shoulder. Slightly startled, I turned around.

Standing behind me was a woman, a little taller and a little older than me. She said, "I thought you might be cold, so I brought you a jacket. I'm Emily."

She draped the jacket around my shoulders.

"I didn't realize it was cold," I told her. "Thank you." I slipped my arms in the sleeves.

Emily was grinning like we knew one another.

"I didn't think there was anybody else camping beside us," I said.

She pointed toward a tent just a hundred feet across from us, partially tucked away on the edge of the dense forest.

"There are a lot more campers. They're just set up around the parameter, hidden by the trees, or a little deeper in the woods. I'm making pancakes for breakfast, and we'd like to have you join us." Then she pointed a few yards away from her tent to a picnic table, where her husband was sitting. "We'll be over there."

It was too dark to see anything, but I wasn't going to deny the girls pancakes. "Yes, we would like that. Thank you, kindly."

She disappeared, and I returned to my burning log and glowing embers.

The following day with the sun shining brightly, the girls and I went to Emily's campsite and introduced ourselves to our new neighbors. Emily said she had a stack of warm pancakes waiting for little girls to devour. Amelia and Asia weren't shy. They filled their bellies with pancakes and syrup and were ready to dance under the sun. I thanked Emily and her husband, Dan, and began walking away when Dan nodded at Emily as he went back inside their tent. Emily handed me some money, and I was humbled and caught off guard, shaking my head in disbelief.

Emily insisted. "Please, take it, in case you or the girls need something."

I slipped the money into my pocket and softly thanked her, beginning to choke up. Yes, God was with us. Then, as if she hadn't done enough, Emily offered to give us a ride to town if we needed to pick up any supplies.

It was such a beautiful day; I told her I wanted to enjoy the walk instead.

"Thank you both, kindly," I said, giving her a big hug. "If you see a little old lady with sun-kissed silver and gray hair, please tell her a bear didn't get us, we've gone for an adventure, but we'll be back."

Something told me we should go to Boulder, but first, I heard about a campsite with a hot tub near the 31.4-mile-long Boulder Creek. I never heard of a camp that fancy, but it seemed like a great place to soak in nature. By the time we reached that site, it was a little before noon and packed. Taking in the view affirmed the reasons it was the place everyone went camping.

That night, I found three huge flattop rocks by the creek. The girls and I each had a rock to sleep on. We rested under the blanket of the sky with continuous sounds of nature as the lullaby. The temperature seemed so perfect we didn't need anything. There were no blankets, no pillows, and no mosquitoes to disturb the picturesque night. Directly in front of me were breathtaking views of the high cliffs. Between us was an awe-inspiring rustling creek. I was exhausted, but it was too romantic to sleep. I didn't want to miss the imposing beauty begging for my wholehearted attention, so I stayed awake to witness nature dance before me. The lights from the campsites added to the stars, creating a dimly candlelit atmosphere. I absorbed the vibrant colors of the sky changing before my eyes as the clouds drifted into delightful formations. I thought that, although we didn't have a physical house, from my perspective, blanketed in beauty, this was not homelessness. It was phenomenal! I didn't know how to describe such utter beauty, but I was grateful for the experience that filled me with much reverence for nature and its grand designer. I felt connected to my children, Mother Nature, Grandfather, the Universe, and myself. I wanted to see beyond the mountain ridges, and God allowed me to see so much more. In the process, God had given me the freedom to find my place in this world—along with Deja. And I was never alone, as God reminded me: *I am that log burning to keep you company and that woman who put a jacket on you.*

I was still like the cliffs, knowing that this was all God. That was the best sleepless night I ever had, and I watched every moment as the dawn greeted the rising of the sun. I couldn't abandon the majestic beauty—that's what I went there to experience, to fill my soul with, and to heal from. Seek the kingdom of God, and the rest will follow. I was tuning in to who I am, knowing it would lead to my heart's desires. My beautiful girls were in a deep sleep when I wrapped them up and loaded them in the buggy. I hoped that one day, they would find themselves as connected to God and His creation as I was. I wanted them to learn how to be still long enough to appreciate and embrace life's experiences outside of the confines of boundaries. It was cathartic.

At the crack of a peaceful dawn, while the girls were still sleeping, I had pushed the double buggy up along the side of the creek. There were a few men scattered throughout the creek, gracefully fly-fishing. One of them caught a nice one. We made it back to the campsite before eight o'clock, and I went to the reception desk inside the cottage to check to see if any spots were available. The clerk said, "Unfortunately, it's completely full for the entire month. You must have an advanced reservation to get a space."

I thought, *You know the drill; be patient.* So, I went and sat quietly off to the side and waited. After a while, a young couple, who were honeymooning, walked up to the receptionist and told her that they decided to check out, leaving a spot available for the week. As soon as they walked away, I stood back in front of the same receptionist, asking for their spot. And we got it! With the rate she gave me, I had enough to pay for a week at that fancy camp. Of course, the first day was all about soaking up the sun until we turned into prunes.

The second day at the camp, I decided that we'd go check out downtown Boulder and see what kind of job I could find. On the way to the Pearl Street Mall, a four-block pedestrian mall, I came across a halfway house for single mothers in situations like mine. We went inside, and within an hour, we had an apartment with a childcare center within the housing complex. I gave up the camping spot and got the rest of my money back since we stayed for only two days, and we moved into the halfway house. The girls were settled in childcare while I went on job interviews. I applied for the Hotel Boulderado, a five-star hotel and restaurant that was one of the most famous landmarks in Boulder. I didn't have the experience to compete with other applicants who had extensive training. But I applied along with the most qualified of them. Our orientation was hosted in a big hall. Individual interviews followed before the final interview with the general manager, if we made it to that point.

My first interview was with the woman who spoke at the orientation. She was articulate, and I told her, "You have so much charisma." However, she didn't say anything to me now or ask about my work experience, which I didn't have. Since I was going for the interview experience and she wasn't saying anything, I asked her if she'd seen *Gandhi*. I told her she should watch that movie. It was great!

She looked at me and said, "You're going to get a call from the general manager upstairs."

The next day I was face to face with the big general manager.

The interview was short. He didn't ask for my work experience either, and no one asked for my résumé, which was fine by me because I didn't have one. I didn't know what to put on a résumé or how it should look.

When I met the general manager, he asked me two questions.

"Why do you want to wait tables?"

"I like serving food. And one should serve with love."

Then he asked, "When do you want to start?"

I needed that day to adjust to the idea that I just got the job. While talking with the general manager in the restaurant, I saw the waiters hustling. I didn't see myself scurrying around that way, and I wasn't sure if that type of job would work for me. I took my time and enjoyed moments of stillness. But my primary responsibility was providing for my girls, so I told him, "I'd like to start tomorrow."

On the first day of my very first job, I stood staring at the computer screen. Whoever got the job was supposed to know how to do it, so there wasn't any training. I was thrown right into it. Everyone knew the menu inside and out, but I didn't know squat. I knew what eggs were, but I didn't know all the different ways to prepare them. When I managed to take an order, I struggled to input it correctly. I noticed a girl behind me, watching me move as slow as a turtle. I felt her irritation. She had extensive waiting experience in Aspen, and she was attending the University of Colorado Boulder. She could do that job in her sleep. After a while, she couldn't take it anymore.

"I wonder how you got the job?" she said snidely.

I didn't think she meant it as a question.

I turned to face her and calmly replied, "I wonder myself."

I'm sure she thought I was going to karate chop her, but I moved to the side so she could have the computer to herself. I could tell she knew exactly what to do with me. I got through that first day and the first week. Then, just as I was beginning to get the hang of it, I went in one day—and got fired.

Well, at least I got way further than the interview. Not too bad. I stopped in a record store on my way home and bought myself a New Age CD. The girls were still in childcare, so I took the time to relax and listen to it; I loved New Age music. In the middle of getting lost in a trance, the phone rang, but I ignored it and went back to my blissful state. Only it was one of those phones that rang and rang until I'd pick up. Something told me to answer it, so I did. It was a manager from the restaurant, not the one who fired me. I didn't know how many managers worked in that place, but she said she wanted me back as soon as possible, right away. I told her I was in the middle of something and that I'd think about it. She demanded that I'd let her know as soon as possible. I told her, "Okay, as-soon-as-possible is not right now." I didn't particularly appreciate being treated as though I was still disposable and anyone could devalue or disrespect me at will. I went back to my CD, but the phone started ringing again. It was her again, wanting to know if I could come back right away. I knew that I needed to take care of my girls, and I agreed to go back the next day so she'd stop calling and I could enjoy my peaceful trance.

When I entered the restaurant the following day, every table was occupied, and there was a wait. I walked past the girl who was irritated with me, and she looked shocked. She was probably the one who got me fired. Watching her wrestle with her annoyance was worth the return, but I felt I needed to do something that would help me find Deja, and this wasn't it. I went into the manager's office. The one on duty happened to be the guy who fired me.

I said, "Oh, hey there! I'm not feeling this position. I think I'd be better off in the food prep. By chance, is there an opening there?"

"No," he said, looking at me flatly.

"Okay," I said. "If I quit, how much notice do you need?"

"Three weeks."

"Three weeks! You didn't give me three seconds when you fired me. How about two weeks?"

That week, I found another job at a Japanese restaurant prepping food, and the pay was even better. The first three months, all of my coworkers were trying to get a raise. But the owner wouldn't give anyone a penny more. I knew they needed the help. I was working hard and doing a good job, so I took a different approach with him.

"Listen, I wanted to let you know I'm not going to be able to work much. Maybe just one or two days a week, or I can just sub for others."

He pulled me aside and asked, "How much of a raise do you want? I've never seen anyone roll sushi the way you do it."

"I've never rolled sushi before. It's just that I enjoy it," I said, appreciating the compliment.

◇◇◇◇◇◇◇◇◇◇◇◇

I must have left Berkeley with a crater-sized hole because Drake noticed I was gone. After I got the job at the Japanese restaurant, he showed up at my door with his Bentley—Cathy. She brought gifts for the girls and me. Her arms were wide open. For the first time, I felt her warmth. I'd never felt so wanted. I was like a discarded child she found in some mound full of garbage. Then, she made me an offer.

"Why don't you and the girls live with me? Save some money. You don't have to pay rent." She took my hands like a mother would when pouring her heart out to her child and pleaded with me. But, of course, the rent-free part was the Mafia offer.

"Drake is the beat of my heart. I'll do anything to make him happy."

Maybe she got to me because I missed Mama, and I craved the type of love she was showing her son. It seemed that something was off, but she was an accountant, and indeed she had it under control.

Something about her caused a deep unconscious void to bubble to the surface so I could face myself, blast through the darkness, and forever shed light on the black hole I had inside. The part where Cathy said, "He's the beat of my heart" reverberated in my consciousness. Since I was a little girl, I had wanted to feel that deep love. I wanted it from her too. I felt that way with Amelia and Asia, but I never had anyone feel that way about me.

I was ready for something normal. My life was pieced together, and outside of nature, I couldn't feel what I needed. I used to wonder if I would ever have a family who loved me so much that I would never have to search for love again. At some point, I started feeling like I was living from box to box. The box got bigger, but it was still a box. When I moved into a new one, it was only a matter of time before I'd outgrow it, which left me suffocating. That's why I craved fresh air and nature. It was the only place I felt safe. That suffocating feeling warned me when it was time to leave.

Before we left Berkeley, I told Drake that we were heading up to Colorado. I was hoping he'd say, "Yes, I want to go with you," but I wasn't going to hold my breath. Good thing I learned how to breathe on my own. I scared the shit out of that boy when I said those three words, *moving to Colorado*. Some people are scared of snakes, spiders, and heights, while others are scared of success, and some are scared shitless of words. And so I had to let him go.

A few months later, just as my daughters and I were getting

settled in Boulder, that's when Drake and Cathy reappeared. I never knew how badly I wanted to be loved, but strangely, Cathy also wanted to be loved just as much. We both were searching outside of ourselves to feel love.

7.

Roses from an Officer and a Gentleman

WHEN I GAVE MY TWO-WEEK NOTICE AT THE JAP-anese restaurant, my boss thought I was scheming to get another raise.

Again, he pulled me aside and asked, "How much do you want for a raise?"

"Thank you, but no raise. I'm moving to Connecticut for vocational rehabilitation and to go to school."

Cathy caught a flight back to Connecticut while Amelia, Asia (who were now five and two, respectively), and I drove cross-country with Drake. The five-day trip filled with plenty of conversation made me feel closer and more trusting of him. And my girls seemed comfortable with him. We even made some fun stops at places along the way for sightseeing. When the girls fell asleep in the back seat, Drake helped carry them into the motel.

For once, I felt I wasn't alone, and I didn't have to ask for help. It was refreshing.

It was early evening when we finally arrived at his mother's house in Greenwich. They lived in a nice neighborhood, in a two-story house. Beyond the big imposing front door was a high-ceilinged living room, making the space feel open and big. A perfectly dimmed crystal chandelier dramatically glistened over the glass dining table. Upstairs were two bedrooms; one for Drake and me and the other for the girls. Cathy had filled their closet with new clothing. She even had their bedding and pillows embroidered with their names.

Drake and Cathy made us feel comfortable, like we fit, from the onset. We made dinner together, ate together, and said grace before anybody had a bite. It felt like home. I had wanted a normal life for the girls. I didn't want them to experience any of my trauma or feel unloved. I desperately wanted my girls to be safe and loved in a healthy environment—although I didn't know what that was yet. I didn't grow up in one, and I didn't know how to create it, but I thought this could be it—what I'd seen on television, a family together, eating, laughing, and happy. Drake and Cathy seemed to give me something I was searching for, but that void inside remained.

Amelia started grade school and got into the gifted program. Asia started pre-K. Things were progressing, and I got a job working at an office where I helped transcribe Cathy's reports. I wanted Cathy to know how much I appreciated living with her and being treated as a part of her family. I wanted to contribute to show her that I wasn't a freeloader.

Over time, Cathy and I grew close, like mother and daughter. I didn't feel loved by my mother and family, which had a lot to do with my search, and I learned that Cathy was just as starved for love as I was. We gave each other the love we never felt we received. I couldn't quite understand how someone so successful couldn't keep her family together enough to feel loved, especially when her job was to solve problems. But then again, her profession didn't mean she was perfect. Cathy had two kids with serious personal issues. She confided in me that she never felt truly loved by them. Her husband had passed away long ago. Since then, Cathy became married to her job. Given all the time she spent confiding in me, as well as her grandmotherly relationship with Amelia and Asia—my new name for Bentley was Mother.

After our typical graceful chandelier family dinners, Drake would play with Amelia and Asia while Mother and I would clear the table. We'd chat in her bedroom while she'd chug a few glasses of Chablis while regurgitating stories and situations she'd heard from clients throughout the day. I'd listen with curiosity, all the while rubbing her feet as if the Chablis wasn't enough to shut down her overstimulated sympathetic nervous system. It fascinated me to no end. It was therapeutic knowing that I wasn't the only one fucked up.

There had always been an emotional distance between my biological mother and me. Now, there was also a great geographical distance as well. Perhaps to compensate for that missing relationship, I cared for Mother the way I should have cared for my biological mother. I wanted to do something special for her, so I decided to help her with dating. Since she didn't have time to meet men and go out on dates, I helped her make time for online dating. I posted pictures of Mother that I'd taken to make sure the framing was perfect. The online dating profile headline read, *Professional female, kind, loving, a great cook, and most of all A+++ in bed looking for true love.* I didn't want Mother to be alone. Hopelessly romantic, I was seriously desperate for her and chatted with several quality studs who I was sure would shatter Mother's earth and make her heart throb. I narrowed the selection to one. His name was Albert. He looked like Richard Gere in *An Officer and a Gentleman*, complete with salt-and-pepper hair. Albert was a successful entrepreneur who was taking time off to find the love of his life. After three months of online conversation, Albert decided it was time to meet face to face. He was falling madly in love with Cathy. Rather, it would be more accurate to say he was falling in love with me since I was the one corresponding with him. Still, I was excited for Albert and Cathy to finally meet. Throughout the courtship, I kept Mother briefed on everything I said to Albert and vice versa, and I couldn't wait to see Mother's face when she looked into Albert's eyes.

The day I scheduled them to meet, Cathy got dressed up. She looked quite beautiful. When the doorbell rang, I eagerly dashed to open it and welcomed Albert. He was dressed nicely and held a bouquet of perfect roses. After I gracefully introduced Mother, she shook his hand and said, "Hello."

Albert replied, "It's a pleasure to meet you, Cathy, finally." He handed Cathy the bouquet of roses while sizing her up, head to toe. In a matter of seconds, something zapped the hell out of Mother's brain—anxiety, a sense of terror, another personality, or something beyond my comprehension because a cold, calculated demeanor took over.

She turned to me, stating quite callously, "This is Deja. She's the one writing to you."

Cathy quickly and intentionally shattered the painstakingly hard work I'd done on her behalf for three months. When Albert looked at me, I couldn't read his face. Embarrassed, I looked at him with a blank expression while experiencing a few rapid synchronized blinks.

"I hope you understand I meant well," I confessed.

"Of course. It's nice to meet you, Deja," he said forgivingly.

"I'm sorry, Albert," Mother added sharply before walking away.

"Well, I'd better get going. I have a meeting in town," were Albert's last words on his first visit.

In that brief, intense moment, I realized that everyone wants love, but very few understand what it means to want love. Albert and Cathy taught me that to solicit love, one must first understand what love means, beyond all human conditioning, social or otherwise. And that understanding takes effort. Conscious effort. It requires us to get off autopilot mode and take the initiative to look inside and understand what we are asking for before we can connect with others. Chances are great in matching up with someone alike once we've done the self-inquiry. That takes a great deal of work—essentially, it involves looking at ourselves, which can be pretty mind-boggling or just plain frightening. We might not like what we see, which means we would expose ourselves for others to see us too. Cathy wasn't willing to do that, which made me wonder what she was trying to hide.

It's easier to look at others and see what we don't like. And with that same mindset, that's a way of distracting ourselves from looking at who we are and changing anything we don't like. Deliberate deflection is damaging to ourselves and others. It holds us back and closes us off from experiencing the possibilities.

The afternoon continued with Mother pretending nothing happened. Technically she was right because nothing happened. She gave me the bouquet of roses to recognize my efforts and said, "He should have given you these flowers," then went into the pantry and poured herself a full glass of Chablis.

I appreciated Mother for keeping all her chickens together in one coop. I could tell she was trying hard. Almost too hard.

There was much more to her story than I knew, and it was concerning. But I dismissed it.

Mother always had big ideas, and one of them was when she told me to adopt her last name.

I didn't want to change my name, so I flippantly said, "No, but maybe by marriage."

That backfired because then she wanted to plan the wedding. It didn't matter that Drake hadn't even proposed. She insisted that we start planning our wedding, so I could get her last name, while Drake was busy smoking weed with his buddies. When Drake came home as high as he could get, it triggered in me a deep concern coupled with anger. We were close, but when Drake was deep-red-eyed high, he seemed like a different person and I didn't want him around my girls.

Contemplating my triggers had become a pastime. I desperately wanted Drake and Cathy to be the complete and loving family I needed, but something wasn't adding up. I wanted my girls to have a grandma and a daddy, but the more I reflected upon the situation the more I realized that I was setting the bar too low. Is that really what I wanted for my children? I didn't know how I hit such a low level and was willing to settle for so little.

Trying to fit in with society was damaging me. It was unnatural and hard on my nervous system, creating a vicious fight-or-flight cycle. I still didn't know where the hell love came from, even with the lessons Drake and Cathy were teaching me.

Our dynamic had always been a little dysfunctional, but it had worked well enough. I began paying closer attention to things. In particular, the way Mother doted on Drake reminded me of something I never got. I began to sense that my closeness with Mother threatened Drake. One day we had a silly fight over peanut butter and broke up. I don't know why it had to be peanut butter, but the message was clear: I was insignificant to him. Ultimately, Drake confessed his feelings and told me, "You only wanted to be with me because of my mother. You've gotten as attached to her as she was with me!"

I didn't need Cathy, but I did need a mother's love. With conditions, Cathy did provide me with the kind of love I craved. Drake was right to feel that I only wanted him for his mother; I was trying to fill that painful void somehow.

8.

The Deafening Silence

'D BEEN THINKING ABOUT MY FAMILY BACK IN THE village, most likely because it was time I did. I'd never left them, though, because they were always with me. The smell of Mama on her pillow, resting in fruit trees, magical sunrises, and the mysterious mountain ridges. I missed Mama and my siblings, so I told Mother, "I want to go see them." It seemed respectful to discuss it with her first, and surprisingly, she agreed that it was a good idea for me to go home. I hadn't been back to the Philippines in five years, and I thought it would be best if I made that trip alone. I didn't want to call and tell anyone I was coming. I knew I'd have to explain why I had been out of contact for so long and thought it would be better to do it in person, so I decided to show up unannounced, like the ghost I'd become. Mother agreed that it was best to leave Amelia and Asia with her and Drake.

My relationship with Drake and his mother brought me to a place where I needed to reconnect with my family. I'd had to leave home and go through everything I went through. I just needed time to get my shit together and be in my own space while in the process, but now it was time to reconcile with my past. Being ready to see my family meant I was prepared to face the truth about myself. I discovered a continuous expanding process. One I've learned to embrace. Leaving home was about me, and my return was too. I had to acknowledge that I was no longer afraid of even seeing my molesters. I had to accept that I had grown past that fear, and their ability to hurt me was long gone. I was taking back the power they had stolen from me. I was returning to the place I hated because I feared it. With Mama, Papa, my brothers, and sister, nothing or no one could make me feel safe—but me.

In different ways, Socrates, Jesus, Mother Teresa, Rumi, and the other great mystics and thinkers of all time taught the same thing: "Know thyself." No, I don't mean me as in poor me. I mean the divine *self*—the source of everything. My journey was far from over. It was the expansive journey of becoming.

◇◇◇◇◇◇◇◇◇◇◇

On the flight, I felt anxious. I didn't know how the trip was going to begin or end. I wanted to just show up and say, "Hey, I'm here, and I'm doing great," like a cat that had fallen off a five-story building and landed on its feet. But that's not what happened.

When I landed, no one came to the airport to pick me up because no one knew I was there. I caught a motorcycle cab straight to my parent's rental apartment. I sneaked into the studio with the hidden key. I wasn't worried about getting in because sometimes we didn't bother locking up. There was nothing to steal. I turned the key in disbelief that I had returned.

"Hello? Is anybody home?" I said, poking my head inside.

No one answered, so I went in and looked around. The studio was small but tidy, with a kitchen and dining table. The space could fit seven or eight people, standing. I laid down on the bottom bunk, pooped from the thirteen-hour flight, and slept for about two hours. It was midafternoon when I awoke from my nap; I thought Mama should have been home by then because she'd have to make dinner. Still tired, I drifted back to sleep until the sound of footsteps in the hallway woke me. My heart started pounding as a young couple walked in, carrying grocery bags. They were as surprised as I was—and their faces said it all.

"What! Who the fuck are you?" the guy asked, with an American dialect spilling out of his dropped jaws. After a long second, I gathered myself and apologized. I told them my parents used to rent this particular apartment unit. They looked at me like I had just interrupted their honeymoon. Then, petrified, I jumped up, apologizing profusely for invading their space, steadily explaining my predicament as I grabbed my bag, slipped between them and out the door. I'd been away for so long I didn't even know where my parents were!

I was back home and didn't know where home was. I decided to try Sissy. The last I heard, she was renting a room at my aunt's place. The town was small, but it still took me a while to make my way to my aunt's. I finally made it and stood quietly in front of the property, watching my sister sweeping the porch with a fat broomstick made out of coconut stalks—the same broomstick Mama used to beat me with before she got involved with the church and became the pope of the village. I didn't want to startle Sissy, so I waited for her to notice me. I thought of the experiences I was having in America. Even when

I was temporarily homeless with my girls, it wasn't comparable to the pigsty she was living in, which weighed heavily on my heart. America, the land of milk and honey, the land of opportunity, beyond the mountain ridges, was helping me discover more to life and more to me. My sister glanced in my direction and stopped sweeping. She held the broomstick while staring at me. I knew she was unsure whether it was me.

As memories and emotions flooded back, I was glad that I hadn't brought Amelia and Asia. I was facing a painful past, and I didn't know how I'd respond. No mother would want their children to experience what I had. But it was up to me to become strong enough to face my past so I could discover the best version of myself—the person I was destined to be. The emotional trauma and memories I carried prevented me from being who I am and seeing my true potential. I needed to remove the fear, release anything that wasn't serving me, and live wholly. In part, I think my journey was about emancipating myself from history and starting fresh. That encompassed letting go of the limiting belief of *unworthiness* and beating myself up. That's why nature was such a big part of me. It was fresh—and every day was a new start.

I could tell by my sister's face that she, too, was confused. Sissy looked as though she was about to beat me up with the broomstick, and at the same time, pick her little sister up and twirl her around, but she couldn't make up her mind. I should have brought her a gift because that may have helped. When Sissy ran toward me, I'd never seen her so angry and happy at the same time. I was ready to accept whatever she was feeling and hold the space to let her respond since I was the one MIA. Maybe I should have told her I was coming, but I didn't want to explain anything. Besides, it would have cost as much as a plane ticket to explain via long-distance phone call how I married for the wrong reason and the journey that followed to unfuck myself.

I stood still, ready for anything, but she only jokingly pre-
tended to hit me with the broomstick, as happy to see me as I
was seeing her. I had nothing but gratitude for that moment
because she had nothing to do with my leaving.

It was getting dark, and the whole town was shutting down
for the day. Sissy told me that shortly after I left, our parents
returned to the barrio where we grew up. We found a car to
take us. The driver wanted a lot of money. Since we didn't have
another option, I agreed to pay. The drive was uncomfortable.
There weren't any streetlights, and the driver hit several potholes passing through various barrios that were all quiet and shut
down for the night. There still wasn't any electricity, but I could
see a few kerosene lamps flickering. Most people had gone to
bed by six o'clock, the same time as the chickens—years later,
everything seemed the same, while things change every day in
America, especially technology.

Everything was quiet when we got to the village. Sissy instructed the driver where to stop. Even in the dark, I could tell
the place was beyond repair, needing to be completely torn down
and rebuilt from the ground up. Walking up to my parents' front
door, I imparted a welcomed sadness. After a few steps inside,
I stood still and waited while my sister went to wake Mama.
It was surreal to hear Sissy in Mama's room, telling her, "She's
here." It sounded strange. When Mama entered the room, she
must have thought she was dreaming when she saw me standing
in front of her. My eyes watered, and my heart dropped—Mama
had lost so much weight, and I felt to blame. She never stopped
praying for me.

Papa was always working, but this time he was there sleeping
too. Only, when Papa's eyes met mine, I don't think he knew
what was going on because he froze and then went back into

the room. Maybe Papa was trying to wake himself up, thinking he saw my ghost. I hoped I didn't give him a heart attack and thought I shouldn't have shown up after five years without telling them. They had consulted a psychic to see if I was still alive, Mama said. "The psychic told us you were alive—just going through a major transition," which provided them with a bit of relief.

Their house was small, and the conversation woke my two brothers. My older brother was pretty mellow, a happy-go-lucky dude, but if there was one person in the world who could get on my nerves, it would be my youngest brother. We both liked arts and crafts, so he would steal my stuff, which drove me crazy.

Unsolicited memories continued to bombard me while we engaged in conversation. It became awkward and strange, like I had done something that upset everybody and didn't know why. Finally, I sat down, and my youngest brother sat across from me. His demeanor told me that he was in the courtroom, and I was on defense. He was about to let me have it. I always thought he'd make a good lawyer. Given I didn't return to fight and cause drama, he'd succeed in finding me guilty in whatever charges he had in his head. Then he opened his big mouth, and it started yapping and barking like he had a megaphone up to his mouth. He had a lot on his mind. I didn't know what else to do, so I just took it. It was late, I was unannounced, and everyone was entitled to their feelings. To them, I had abandoned my family, but they didn't know what was happening to me and what I had endured for years. For some, it's instinctive to keep something like sexual abuse inside. It's tough to talk to your mama and papa about sex, and it's more difficult and traumatic to tell them anything like that happened to you. I didn't know if they would blame or hate me for speaking up. I didn't know if that was normal for girls. We lived in a small village, and it wouldn't take much for people to gossip about it. But after years of that shit, it wasn't easy to stay quiet. Silence takes courage.

My dear brother ranted about how I put everyone in such massive distress for going MIA. He didn't know that I had lived in tremendous grief living with that pain and the fear of abuse happening again and again. He was so upset about everything that his veins were popping and his face was red. This verbal thrashing from my brother in front of the rest of my family brought about a revelation. Growing up, I thought no one even knew of my existence, so therefore no one would notice that I was gone. But there are two sides to everything, and they, too, had theirs. I was growing in that moment. I kept my pain to myself, and without defending myself, I let him have his opportunity to express what he needed to get out because I saw myself in him. He needed to be heard as much as I did when I was a child.

He started to cry toward the end of his thrashing (or deposition). Later, I found out he had to quit prelaw because my parents couldn't afford the tuition. My absence seemed to cause everyone to focus so much on the grief I caused them that they hadn't bothered to ask how I was doing. It was like a massive, cleansing storm pouring down, and it passed because storms go away.

By the time we got through everyone's grief, it was almost time for the chickens and roosters to begin their performance and my chance to break my lifelong silence and tell them my side of the story. I had to balance everyone's emotions so they didn't continue to view me the way they had. I spoke up before all was lost. It hurt, but I told them—and it brought another storm where everyone shed tears. The storm cleared before the sun rose, and the words were said to offer healing for anyone who wanted it, myself included. Telling them what had happened to me, my truths, and what I'd been through helped me understand that I mattered—to them and to me, which was the reason everyone fell apart over my disappearance. At breakfast, we all sat together, and my mother led us in grace. We'd said everything that needed to be said. Silence was the main course. I compared it to the Last Supper, except no one was crucified; instead, it was the resurrection. I never knew just how much grace there was until I saw behind Mama's distressed face and through everyone's grief. I was deeply grateful to see beyond the facade and beneath the surface of the mundane.

While contemplating how I would create closure on that part of my journey, someone knocked on the door. Through the holes in the wall, I saw one of my abusive relative's wife. She was freaking out because her husband was ill, and he needed to be rushed to the hospital, a six-hour boat ride. My dear family member was crying because she couldn't afford the boat fare. They lived a few houses away, so I went to see him. He was a mere skeleton puking blood. The sight of him alone opened my heart to offer forgiveness that I didn't know I had or hadn't thought possible to acquire. I reached into my pocket and handed him a couple of hundred-dollar bills. It wasn't small change, especially since it was someone who hurt me. But that day, they rushed him to the hospital. After a short recovery period, he died.

Growing up, I'd often go with my sister to gather firewood. I thought we'd go for a walk in the woods to check out how the landscape had taken on a different shape than I remembered. We passed by a small unfinished house made of bamboo and coconut straws. Sissy said we should stop by and say hello. It was the home of another relative who abused me. Even though he was the one who had abused me the most, I agreed. I wanted to look at him to see if I could forgive him. He wasn't quite sitting nor standing because it turned out that he had some serious health condition. He looked uncomfortable. We didn't stay long, just long enough for my heart to vomit forgiveness. The forgiving wasn't for him. It was for me—so I could move forward in balance in a healthier manner and with a lighter soul, free of the history that was impossible to change. It was a psychic detox. I came to understand that I can change the way I look at a situation and see something that creates possibilities and opens my heart. I didn't have any money left in my pocket. Forgiving him was more than enough, and generous at that.

Sissy and I walked across city blocks of rice paddies where I used to run along the narrow water irrigation canal. A guy in a faded long-sleeved shirt and a straw hat was weeding in the middle of the field. My sister said hello to him, and my forehead scrunched together while I had the thought that I knew that guy. I stopped right in front of him. I wanted him to look at me, but he couldn't, and I felt his fear. He couldn't consciously bring himself to do it. The man acting as though he'd catch on fire was the third abuser. I watched him move away from me—a dead man. There was nothing but fear and the imprisonment of its phantom and haunting existence. I had no words for what God was showing me. While it seemed those who abused me got past me, they didn't get past God.

The visit home was overwhelming—my reintroduction to my family and seeing my three molester relatives without speaking a word. The visual alone reflected my growth and healing. I released that toxicity from my system by forgiving myself. Forgiving them was hard, but then I was able to look at myself and them and say, "This has made me stronger and wiser. You didn't break me; it devoured you." The adversity only made me realize my strength and resilience, something I would need on my journey. I was over blaming myself for their transgressions, thinking I'd done something wrong or committed an unforgivable sin deserving of punishment. If I continued to carry that negative past, I would have continued suffering.

My adverse history didn't serve me, so I released it. I forgave Mama because she didn't know what had transpired, and I hadn't given her the chance to make it right because I never told her. She couldn't stop what she didn't know was occurring. I never told her when it began. I lived in a society where women are devalued and raised to be silent, to be submissive, and to hold whatever shit they are given. And it was still that way in America. Unknowingly, I was teaching my children to do the same. When we are silent, we teach our children to be the same. Yes, it took courage to sustain that silence, but that was wrong. *I should have used that courage to speak out.* Suppose women were encouraged to speak out against what isn't safe and doesn't feel right. In that case, the things that hold us emotionally hostage would cease to damage us. The opportunity to change my path would have begun sooner had I only spoken out. It may not have changed what initially took place, but it may have prevented its hold on me moving forward.

When I returned to Connecticut, I closed that door and opened myself to receive all the blessings, grace, and freedom given to me as my birthright. What was important was not what happened but what I did with the adversity. That would ultimately determine the outcome of my journey and be the reality of my own making.

9.

Deja Vu

THE BOEING AIRCRAFT WAS STILL VIBRATING IN MY head after I landed. The aftermath of that intercontinental flight was comparable to an elephant running over me and leaving me in a momentary comatose state before finally making it back to my girls, Drake, and Mother. Just seeing them made me feel like I stepped out of a time machine.

Everything *appeared* the same, but instinctively, I *sensed* somehow it was different. The massive jet lag hitting me on top of everything that occurred in the Philippines caused me to dismiss what I intuitively sensed. I was looking forward to normal, but once I was back I realized I didn't want any part of *normal*. What is and who is normal anyway?

For years, I had dysfunctional people taking up space inside my head rent-free, disrupting my body and emotions. But I had started vacating their asses, and I wasn't done. Seeing my family in that dramatic fashion allowed the painful truth to boil to the surface, providing clarity, bringing closure so I could start cleaning up the mess. Something in me shifted, and I didn't know how that shift would play out. But what I did know is that I was learning to be present so I could be aware when things unfolded.

Drake and Mother left for a weeklong retreat in upstate New York, and I was thrilled to be alone with Amelia and Asia. The three of us had a special chandelier dinner and everything seemed perfect. But when I tucked them in bed, Asia said to me, "Mommy, I don't want to live without you." A haunting voice echoed in my conscience, turning my stomach into knots. I tried to be dismissive, thinking it was because I had been gone for two weeks and she missed me terribly, but that wasn't it. I detected that same fear in Amelia's eyes, but she didn't say anything because she didn't want me to feel bad that I left them for that long. I knew that seed of thought was planted in her—*in them*—because my girls didn't talk like that, and they didn't have reason to think that way. Drake, Cathy, Amelia, and Asia had a dialogue about me while I was gone, and it was something significant enough to cause concern that there would be a separation from me. Why? Were they planning something that I wasn't aware of? Something didn't feel right. My girls weren't the same, which meant something changed them while I was gone.

The pressing on my chest was hard, and I needed space to process it. Haunting thoughts of what my relatives had done disturbed me greatly, and they precipitated my wanting to leave Connecticut, to think that same thing could happen here. But how? That wasn't possible. What transpired on my first visit back to the Philippines had a profound effect on my psyche and more than I could begin to admit, and I began to realize that what I thought I had in Connecticut was more like a staged play. That the facade of Drake, Cathy, and family wasn't real. My family was in the Philippines—not here. I wanted my girls and myself to be connected to love, but what they offered wasn't it—it was simply a smoke screen. After Asia's haunting words, I wanted to pack up and leave.

Around this time, I had a dream that I was working in a morgue. I found myself standing amid an endless pool of dead bodies. I was as still as they were, trying to understand why I was even there. It dawned on me that there wasn't anything to do there, nor did I want to do anything. With that clear understanding, my body lifted off the ground, levitating higher and higher, flying high at the speed of light, westbound to California from Greenwich. When I landed in a foothill, I told myself it would be too easy to land on the mountaintop. It'd be more sensible and adventurous to land in the foothills and walk my way to the top—that way, my lungs could acclimate to the altitude. Every step of the way, I felt my lungs expand, adjusting to the elevation. And then there I stood, tall, my spine elongated, on the mountaintop, inhaling and exhaling deeply as much as my expanded lungs could contain. I was planting a flag, just like Neil Armstrong had done on the moon, except mine was a flag with just one star. I thought I'd go down and help people come up so they could plant their flags too.

Greenwich was a fully manicured and pedicured place where every day seemed like a casual Sunday. People there were retired or laying low, living off their loads of trust funds. The city had beautiful beaches and several golf courses. But that stopped resonating with me after a while. I needed different days of the week because having Sunday every day felt lifeless. Besides the looming thoughts of my childhood trauma, Mother's imposing control regarding what she wanted me to do with my life, which revolved pretty much around her and Drake, was now suffocating me. With them, I had lost and released some of my independence. Since returning from the Philippines, hearing Mother's list of everything on her daily agenda did nothing more than irritate a deep wound I thought was healing. Her to-do list sounded much like Harvey's sexually entitled demands. Both were suffocating.

Mother and I were in our matching aprons cooking veggies and fish. She loved baking pineapple au gratin and got me so hooked that I'd beg to have that pie for dessert. That evening the girls had set the table while Drake was in our bedroom rapping with his keyboard synthesizer. He wasn't quite sure if he'd make it in the music industry, but he would have loved to be the next Bob Marley. Mother, the girls, and I sat down for dinner, and Drake came down to join us. The girls rushed through their carrots and peas to get to dessert. I had a lot on my mind that evening, so I skipped dinner altogether. I didn't have an appetite, but I forced myself to eat some of the pineapple au gratin. I didn't want Mother to think anything was wrong. I felt I managed to do a good job concealing my distance. I wasn't the only one that wasn't quite the same; *everyone* seemed out of it or different for some reason. The awkward atmosphere was palpable and weighed heavily on me.

After dinner, the girls went up to their room to change into their jammies, brush their teeth, and get ready for bedtime. Drake returned to his synthesizer and buried himself deep with heavy-duty, noise-canceling headphones. Mother and I were still sitting at the table with a flickering votive candle in the center when I calmly dropped the bomb.

"Mother, I'm going to Los Angeles—without Drake."

Looking at me intently, Mother stopped chewing and turned red—seething—while chugging down a half-full glass of Chablis.

"What about the girls?" she asked.

That was a question? What was I missing?

"They're going where their mother is going. Don't worry. I'm not asking for child support or anything." I was hoping to neutralize her blood pressure with that reassurance.

"I want a *will* stating I have full custody of the girls in case something happens to you!"

Hearing that made me feel like *I* had chugged a whole bottle full of Chablis and was feeling red and seething myself. What the fuck was going to happen to me? *Cool it*, I said to myself, despising the idea that someone could bring this anger out of me. To snap myself out of it, I threw a whole glass of water in my face in a splash. Mother went from being so red she started turning blue from my reaction. What did she think I'd do, leave my girls?

While she stared at me with piercing eyes, I told her, "It's just water. Anyway, I'm not going to die because I can't think of anybody worthy of my children."

Her expression made it clear that if I left, that would be it. We would never have anything to do with each other. But for the life of me, I couldn't see myself staying in this triad. It didn't feel right. At that point, I didn't understand my strong urge to leave them and that place with such urgency. I knew I had to go, and only then would I understand the reasons because there were several—I didn't know what they were yet.

The feeling of suffocation engulfed me, indicating that I was in a box with the top tightly sealed. If I paid attention, my body sent signals alerting me to break out of that box so I could breathe. And if I felt I was in a box and couldn't breathe, how were my girls affected? That thought let me know it was time. I learned to be okay with running away when necessary, and this felt necessary. I could see a mile away when someone or something was going in the wrong direction. I figured out what I wanted, which wasn't something I could buy; it was something

I needed to live—a healthy, loving, and balanced life, not just a house. What I needed was in another direction. It wasn't there—with Drake and Cathy.

Drake warned me, "Don't move to Los Angeles. You could die from an earthquake."

"Don't kid yourself," I replied. "You could die of anything anywhere."

In his fear, that was the best thing he could come up with. The reasons it was time to leave started bubbling to the surface.

That spring of 2000, my girls and I packed a small U-Haul van with our things and headed to Los Angeles.

Once we got on the freeway and crossed the border to New York, then New Jersey, I felt a deep sigh of relief. We drove the most direct route to Los Angeles, stopping only for gas and bathroom breaks along the freeway and at a Best Western or Motel 6 if it felt safe. We didn't take any sightseeing detours. The endless, mostly desolate freeways became a deep cleanse for my beaten-up soul, and I took refuge in the most dramatic and colorful sunset I'd seen spreading in the ever-revealing horizon. Keeping company with deep silence had become familiar. I had become the prodigal son, and silence had its arms outstretched to welcome me back from a long, treacherous journey. Nothing could possibly take my attention from my return. No need for sightseeing. That was the sight and the seeing.

As the girls soaked in this atmosphere, I noticed that when they saw I was okay, they appeared to be okay. This was a vacation—a break from all the drama and unnecessary noise. They never asked for anything and were perfectly fine with whatever we had day to day, which was each other. And that was everything.

◇◇◇◇◇◇◇◇◇◇

Not long after our return to California and settling in our apartment, I found my niche as a masseuse, securing a job with decent pay at a major-league spa, Club Meridian in Century City. The beginning was rough, as I had to get all my nerves primed. I realized there was only one way to be strong—take back my power by standing up and muscle through any triggers. I retrained my faculties and nerves to respond to the situation rather than reacting to past trauma. To respond with grace and deliberate intention. The power comes from calmness. It's effortless and graceful.

My boss sent me on house calls for members, mostly wealthy Hollywood men. Since I was new in town, I didn't know any of them, but that didn't matter; my boss expected me to make the clients happy and get them hooked. Sometimes I let my naivete get the best of me—other than an excellent massage, I didn't know exactly how to please these people since there was no training.

Through word of mouth, my clientele grew, and I got a young couple in their midthirties as a referral. The man had a construction company, and his wife didn't need to work. When I went to their house, I'd set up the table in the spare room directly across from their bedroom. I always worked on the wife first, then her good-looking and successful husband, Allen. Apparently, he had erectile dysfunction up until one day when he laid on my table. Allen was lying on his back while I worked on his hip joint. Suddenly he had a massive erection. He was so thrilled he couldn't contain himself. Well, I wasn't looking, but I couldn't miss it. It made a giant tent the size of the Taj Mahal. Allen thought it was a miracle and that I had the magic hands to restore such dubious talent, and he wasn't shy about it either. He *told* me to do something about it.

I replied, "Allen, I am not here for this, and besides, you

couldn't afford me. Your wife is beautiful! I'd be banging her if I were you!" Allen started pouring his little heart out, telling me he's not getting *something*. "Well, Allen," I said, "I'm clearly not here to give *you* something. If you're not getting something, *you* must be doing something wrong. I have to go. You have to get off my table. Why don't you take a cold shower and jack off?"

Deep inside, I thanked him for that opportunity. I didn't know I had the strength to stand up to someone like that and reclaim my power. It was crucial to understanding how far I'd come, having gone through sexual trauma. So rather than get bent out of shape, from then on, I promised to speak my truth and have fun in the process. Speaking up for yourself is powerful.

After a year at Club Meridian, I was tired of my boss telling me to keep the clientele happy. I went as far as telling him, "If you want their money, why don't you go do it." That's not what I signed up for, and it brought up triggers from the abuse I suffered as a child.

In 2002, I left and went to a spa in Encino, where I started building a private clientele, but I wasn't making much. Amelia and Asia officially met my family when I took them home that year. I thought about the way Mama and everyone adored the girls and doted on them the entire trip. The girls loved the Philippines, nature, and my family, but they were shocked by some cultural differences compared to how they lived.

While I continued sending money home to my family, I couldn't tell them what I was doing for a living because I knew they wouldn't understand what I did exactly as a masseuse—in America. I was a skilled and trained masseuse who gave professional massages, nothing more. But unfortunately, most masseuses in the Philippines didn't make a living the way I did. They probably would have thought I was a prostitute, and what they thought mattered because all I wanted was their love and acceptance.

Papa asked what my job was—and where the money was coming from. In the Philippines, what I sent was considered a lot of money. "Papa, I have a job. I work" was all I said, and after that, Papa nor anyone else pressed me about it.

After eighteen months, I took a position at a spa in Santa Monica and exploited my reputation to build a new clientele. I stayed on when the company was bought out. The clients were wonderful, and there was no pimping out. A female celebrity came to the spa to get a massage with me. She was specific and upfront in telling me how to massage her, especially her breast. Never having heard of that particular request—I was speechless. My gut told me it was okay, so I did it for her. When the session ended, I ran to my boss and told her what I had just done. I wanted her to hear the accurate account of what happened, if there were to be another version later. I was relieved to see my boss laughing as hard as she did. When she finally stopped, she promoted me to head therapist.

In between working, I was studying and reading about film-making. Digital filmmaking was having a moment; it gave people a chance to make a film in a nontraditional way. I decided to enroll in a community college to take classes in cinematography and photography and the dynamics of still photography. It tied into directing because it all worked together. I learned about sound, got into screenwriting, and went deeper into the collaboration between actor and director.

◇◇◇◇◇◇◇◇◇◇◇◇

There must have been about eighty to a hundred people taking their citizenship oath that morning in 2006 in downtown

Los Angeles. The girls were in school, so I was alone among my soon-to-be fellow citizens. The whole time my mind ran through all the little steps, jumps, and leaps I took to get where I stood waving a tiny American flag. It was my third attempt. The first time I took the test, I was still living with Harvey. Because he wouldn't let me see the mail, I never received the letter saying I'd failed. And, of course, Harvey didn't bother telling me. The second time was while I was in Greenwich and Drake's mom received the disappointing letter.

The consul was positioned behind a huge solid oak desk, seated calmly in his authority with a towering American flag next to him. He stately declared my American citizenship with a grandiose welcome. He concluded with an offer I'd been itching for. I'd been in America for sixteen years and ten months; this was long overdue.

"Just this once, you can change your name on the house. What would you like it to be?" he asked, holding my blank citizenship certificate ready for my autograph. I didn't know that was an option, but before he changed his mind, in case this was a fluke, I quickly said, "Deja Vu."

The consul smiled in amusement. "Deja Vu? Really?"

"Prem. Last name is Prem. Deja Vu Prem."

He probably thought my choice sounded more like a gentlemen's club than a name, but I didn't care. After the divorce, I'd been contemplating what my name should be. I wanted a name that resonated from the core of my being and reminded me of who I was—something that would wake me from amnesia and remind me why I came into existence. To the consul, I had to clarify, Prem is Sanskrit for *love*. My name would be a constant reminder to remember to love myself. He handed me the certificate to print and sign my new name. Doing so made me feel like a fresh incarnation of my best self in the making. My green card had read "Alien," but not anymore. I pledged allegiance to the flag of the United States of America. I was official! It wasn't until he gave me my signed citizenship certificate that said Deja Vu Prem that I felt official. It was a total rebirth, although I seemed to be rebirthing myself all the time.

◇◇◇◇◇◇◇◇◇◇

My father was a slave. Because no technology was available, with his bare hands he handled thirty-seven acres of a farm owned by his aunt's husband. Papa planted coconut, corn, peanuts, and I guess everything that grows and bears fruit, while living alone with chickens and pigs. During harvest season, he'd load all the crops onto a raft and travel for nearly three hours down a snaky river to sell in the closest town. He simultaneously herded a team of water buffalo. Papa needed them to pull the raft on the way back. Why didn't he get my grandfather's flying dragon to help with this shit? I guess those fancy creatures are not cut out for work. They like being invisible because they don't want to be bothered. All I know is that it hurts my brain to think of what Papa went through; they promised to send him to law school in exchange for slaving his ass off. Day in and day out, year after year, he waited for that promise to be fulfilled, but there was no school and nothing even close. One day, Papa got tired of waiting. Since everything he did, he did quietly, he quietly took off with nothing but the shirt and pants he had on.

Papa took the bus to Ozamis City, about three hours southeast. That's the region where I was born. When he reached the city, there was no one to greet him. Walking door to door, he asked around if anyone had heard of a man named Anastacio. By all accounts of the story, Papa met a relative of Anastacio who heard he was living in that city and owned a mechanic shop.

After sleeping in some quiet corner, Papa came across someone who knew the location of the mechanic shop. Papa waited at the shop until Anastacio came face to face with him—and that man took my father in like his son.

Papa was grateful to have found this man. Anastacio then trained my father on everything he knew about mechanics and manually making all sorts of mechanical parts. Papa worked alongside Anastacio. He gave most of his earnings to Anastacio and his wife, who was like his mother. Although Papa wanted to go to school to study law, he had to work. Since school wasn't an option, Papa devoted himself to mechanics. He excelled at it. Even without a certificate, diploma, or degree, he was recruited by Southern Island Oil Mill, a company that made all sorts of products from coconuts. The company had only one type of massive computer system, and they needed it to work as it was crucial to running the nationwide operation. When it broke down, the company hired special engineers to fix the computer, but no one succeeded. As a last resort, my father's manager approached him about possibly fixing this machine. Papa took the project. For three months, Papa took the machine apart and studied it, looking for any missing parts he might have to make or salvage. He fixed the darn thing. The machine was shipped to the main operation site in the Luzon and Manila regions. The company insisted that my father travel with the computer. Shortly after, my papa was called to the Malacañang Palace to receive the most outstanding worker award. I remember when Papa returned from touring the presidential palace. Beaming with pride, he told us about his experience; but when he spoke, he was very humble. "It's nothing to brag about," Papa said. Papa had a hard life but never complained. He was the most generous man I've ever met, and he gave so much, expecting nothing back.

Late one evening, I received a call from Sissy. Her words

were solemn as she told me there had been an electrical mal-function at Papa's job. He was trying to fix a machine, but it blew up in his face, burning one side of his body and causing other serious complications. His health went into rapid decline for a year, while he was in intensive care. He lost his speech. I couldn't go home to see him in that condition because I was sweating bullets trying to pay for his intensive care expenses. Desperate to ensure Papa could afford medical care, I considered selling my body and cashing in on the offers I received that would allow me to send even more money home. At that point, with Papa fighting to be alive, I lost my sense of shame. The responsibility fell on me, and a sense of guilt overcame me.

I love dreams because they have a way of cutting through the ornamental bullshit. During this time, I dreamed of my father, and in one of those dreams, he said, "You've always kept your integrity on the high end. That makes me proud of you." So I couldn't sell my body. I just kept working and scraping money together from each paycheck.

I finally returned, unannounced, to surprise Papa with a brief visit while he was recovering. When I walked through the door, I was shocked to see what had become of him. He was frail and had lost about forty pounds. When Papa saw me, his dark brown eyes shut as he turned around and started crying. He didn't say a word. Papa went mute for the rest of that afternoon. That evening, we sat together with minimal conversation, and I was able to tell Papa how much I loved him. It was profound to see the way Mama loved Papa.

After I left, Mama and Sissy let me know that Papa started to decline. At some point, he had a mild stroke. I wasn't there, but I worked incredibly hard to pay his bills. After that visit, I saw Papa only on video call in the hospital, but he had lost his speech and we could only look at one another. Then Sissy or

Mama would hold the phone up so he could hear my voice, and Papa, my Papa, would just cry. It was devastating to see him like that. The man I knew was a provider, strong, and always working to take care of us. I could usually sit with Papa and never say a word, and in the silence, we had the best conversations because I heard him even more—and he heard me.

◇◇◇◇◇◇◇◇◇◇◇

After a private workshop, I decided to return to filmmaking because something was still incomplete. That teacher's voice kept looping in my head, saying, "You will never make it as a female and a minority." Coupled with my growing hunger for creativity, that sent my juices flowing again in 2008. Whenever someone told me I couldn't do something, it just made me want to do it even more. So what do I do with a name like Deja Vu Prem? I wrote, produced, acted, directed, and edited my first film.

I created a film about a guy who had three months to live. Sad and lonely, he forged a friendship with a girl he kidnapped, who, in turn, made him face his mortality. I was going for a dramatic and stylish look. Film noir. Minimal to suit my nano-budget. I met a cinematographer fresh out of school. He had a digital single-lens reflex, a compact digital camera perfect for shooting without permits in public places like the beach. Obtaining a permit in L.A. or Santa Monica costs a pretty penny. So what we did was guerilla filmmaking. The guy was searching for a project like mine to build his reel. He was happy to do it without pay and even got one of his buddies to do the sound. The shoot would take only a couple of days. Then I talked to the owner of a newspaper warehouse in the valley, and he allowed me to shoot in the warehouse for one day, but only during the day, since they operated at night.

Blacking out the windows allowed us to control the lighting in a dark space. I found an actor at L.A. Casting to play opposite me for credits. He liked the project so much that he was happy to pay me to play the part. He provided most of the props and even paid for the food.

Since I had a nano-budget, I had to utilize every square inch of my creative brain and stretch it in every direction to execute my vision. There was a scene where the guy had just kidnapped my character. She was in a convertible, unconscious but appearing to be fast asleep, with him driving. My director of photography asked, "How are we going to shoot this?" Usually, it would be an expensive setup because we had to shoot the scene with the car moving, which meant rigging the vehicle with the camera and the camera operator alongside or using special camera-mounting equipment. In essence, we needed a Hollywood budget. The way I set it up was easier and much more fun. I had the director of photography sit on my lap, shooting me, medium shot, while the car was moving with his bum squashing my legs. The footage came out fantastic.

You have to do it yourself if you want something done, especially if you don't have the money. I shot indie style to avoid the need for permits at the beach. I got the film in the can, and then it was time to do postproduction, and the inspiration to push forward came from Papa. I heard him say, "This isn't about me. This is about you coming here to do what you came to do." He was right, so I crashed a filmmaking class, which had a postproduction suite, to get the film done. The problem was that the teacher wouldn't let me stay in his class unless I'd taken the prerequisites, which would have taken two semesters to fulfill. I wasn't doing that. So I took the teacher aside and advised him, "Look, you're going to have to physically throw me out of this class," which I didn't think he would, especially since he saw

I was actively involved in a group project. It would have been disruptive to the group if he had removed me. In no time, I was cutting my film in the edit suite. By the end of the semester in 2009, it was complete and entered into my school's film festival with that same teacher as one of the judges. Not only did I win the best directing category, but he voted for my film.

After receiving the award, the teacher pulled me aside and said, "I still don't think you should have crashed my class."

Nodding in agreement, I replied, "Thank you."

Amelia was graduating from high school, and Asia was still in high school. The best thing about getting that award was hearing my daughters' praise, "We are so proud of you, Mommy," as it tied into the deepest wound I had.

Before then, because of my free spirit and connection to nature, I always wondered if they thought their mother was crazy.

There was an unbearable heat wave in L.A., so Asia and I decided to travel to Vancouver that October for a film festival. On the trip, finding myself restless one morning, I got dressed at 3:00 a.m. and took a stroll around Stanley Park, where I had an epiphany—Papa was going to die. Then, as though he were beside me, I heard him talking to me.

Papa said, "Girl, you might want to go home."

I said, "But why do I need to go home? You're not going to be there?"

"You aren't coming home for me, bozo. You're going home for your mother, sister, and brothers. They need you."

After a week in Vancouver, we left and returned to L.A. for two days. I was preparing to return home when I got a call from Sissy.

She said, "I have to tell you something, but don't get upset." My heart sank, I knew what she was going to say, and she said it: "Papa's gone."

◇◇◇◇◇◇◇◇◇◇◇◇

Amelia had moved out and was in college in 2009, and I stayed busy working. After one particularly difficult session at work, I found myself with tremendous anxiety. Rather than go straight home, I decided to take a long hike in the Santa Monica mountains, thinking it might help. Mentally, I did an inventory of everything I was probably suppressing; I'd never felt that kind of anxiety before. While I was climbing to the top, the thought of my family kept surfacing. I thought how I had been there for them, but I didn't think they had been here for me. Then I wondered why. Realistically, the Pacific Ocean was between us, and I had chosen to relocate to a different continent. But, I thought, that shouldn't stop anyone from caring. So I dug deeper, realizing the reason they hadn't been there for me was that I hadn't given them a chance to. Bingo? Not quite. But I was onto something because, with that truth, the anxiety began to diminish. I continued following that train of thought and went deeper until I hit the root. How was I not giving them a chance? They didn't know what I was going through because I hadn't shared my truth with them. Perhaps I was ashamed of myself and afraid to tell them *who I was*, which created a revelation from a memory with Amelia and Asia several years prior on their way to elementary school. There were many days that I thought of Taylor, my friend from school in the Philippines. Since her, I'd always had an undeniable attraction to women but had never acted on it. That day, avoiding a direct question, I somewhat danced around it and asked my girls, in third person, "How would you feel if your mother was gay?"

I paused, waiting to be bombarded with questions or an unfavorable reaction, but there was none. They were so free about it, giving me the sense it wasn't a problem—at all. They didn't question it, and their love for me wouldn't change. That memory led me to why I was so afraid to tell my family. It was that I hadn't accepted who I was in the first place. And I couldn't expect others to accept something that I hadn't. Finally, the diminishing anxiety was morphing into courage, and I thought, *If I tell my family, they might disown me.* So then what? It was time to let go of the assumptions that created convoluted thinking and fear. I thought running and avoiding my family might just be about one thing—acceptance. *Self-acceptance.* After what my cousin and uncles did to me, I couldn't accept myself as whole or healthy. I was damaged, with those burdens and secrets to carry for the rest of my life. It was so dark that I took them to another country and hid there. I didn't believe my family would accept or love me, especially since I didn't know if they did to begin with—besides, I didn't know what love was or where it came from after what had happened to me.

10.

OMG GROWING THROUGH

B EING A MOTHER WAS SOMETHING I WOULD NEVER
have imagined, but having Amelia and Asia helped me
grow tremendously in such a short period; I'm grateful for
that. But unfortunately, being a single parent catapulted Amelia
into semi-adulthood at just three years old. I can't say I was the
best mother, but they are the best daughters. In many ways, they
raised me.

Amelia has always been calm. Whenever we missed the bus,
she'd constantly reassure me that another was coming. On several occasions, she'd find bills lying around. We were broke and
out of food stamps when Amelia found a fifty-dollar bill in the
bathroom of a grocery store. She just handed it to me with this
look on her face like *There's more where that came from.* She had a
unique way of showing me perseverance, confidence, and faith,
which made me want to push through every time.

Asia is a tricky one. When I did something that required grounding, Asia had a way of provoking my thought process so I'd recognize it—preventing me from continuing to miss the things that mattered. When Asia came home from a rough day at school one afternoon, the first thing I did was order her to do the dishes. Instead, she looked me dead in my face and said, "Why don't you ask me how my day went?" It humbled me, and I felt ashamed. In ways big and small, my girls were my teachers.

Both of my girls were in the gifted program in middle school, taking college-level courses. I couldn't sit with them to do their homework like other mothers did because the course materials were often beyond my level of comprehension. But I was there for them in other ways.

One day, Asia came home from school bent out of shape. She looked like she'd been carrying the whole planet on her shoulders. "I don't like school. I don't connect with anyone," she confessed with a heavy heart.

What could I possibly say to that? I couldn't disagree. While searching for the correct answer, I tried to comfort her.

"Are you hungry? I can make you a tuna sandwich or PB&J."

But Asia wasn't interested in a sandwich. "There's a private school just down the street, about five blocks away," she said. "I'd like to transfer there. The teacher-student ratio is one to one," she added confidently. She'd researched the school. What she didn't take into account was the cost of attendance. Mel Gibson's and Jackie Chan's kids attended that joint, for goodness' sake. The idea was utterly absurd, but I wanted to support my daughter's ambitions, to let her know that there was no limit to what was possible in this life, so I agreed to a meeting with the school principal the next day.

The school didn't resemble a typical school. It was on a block of commercial buildings along Wilshire Boulevard in

Santa Monica. We skipped the tour. We weren't there to evaluate whether the school was good. We already knew that. What appealed to Asia was the low student-teacher ratio. In one class, it would be just her and the teacher, which she liked. The biggest class in that private school had ten to fifteen students. I still didn't know how she'd be able to attend, but I figured it was free to meet with the principal. The principal was easygoing, and she didn't ask many questions. She just sized up Asia and glanced at me.

The whole meeting took no longer than twenty-five minutes. I thought for sure I was hallucinating from hypoglycemia when the principal said, "I'll have all your books and supplies ready first thing in the morning."

I'd been worried about how to convince the principal to allow Asia to attend, but it turned out that I didn't have to convince the principal of anything. There's something about Asia's being. It's that simple. She doesn't whine, demand, or beg. She has a quiet presence, but when she speaks, you feel her heart even if you don't quite understand it.

Direct in her response, Asia told the principal, "I would love it here."

"We would love you here too," she replied, and she offered Asia a *full* scholarship, including books and supplies.

The next day, Asia transferred to that school. It wasn't my blood sugar after all.

The following year, Asia decided to skip high school altogether. When she told me those types of things, I stopped searching for the right words to say and listened instead. She had already done her homework on the matter. She wasn't asking me for permission. There was a problem though. Neither GED nor high school equivalency qualified her to get into college that upcoming year. Asia had found a solution for that as well. There was an exam she could take, and if she passed it, she would skip her last year of high school and go straight to college.

When it came time to take the test, she warned me, "Just so you know, I might not pass this exam because I didn't do any review."

"What? I spent eighty bucks for that review book you didn't even bother to open?"

The following day was a perfect day to be in nature. Amelia was working three jobs while attending UCLA, and I wanted to take Asia's mind off her exam, so I asked her, "Hey, do you wanna go hiking?"

"Can't," she said. "Have to get my class schedule together."

"What class?"

"Oh, didn't I tell you? I passed that exam."

No, I didn't get the memo, I thought.

◇◇◇◇◇◇◇◇◇◇

Both of my girls tried to remove any sort of responsibility from my plate. One day while in high school Amelia came home and told me that she got a job working for Sotheby's.

"Doing what, reception?" I asked.

"Real estate," she replied.

"Don't you have to have a real estate license for that?"

"Yeah, I have one." Unbeknownst to me, she had obtained her real estate license. I never heard her talk about things; she just did them.

Three months later, I asked how she was doing with Sotheby's, and she whimsically replied, "Oh, I don't work for Sotheby's anymore. I work for Keller Williams now."

One day she called me while she was showing an oceanfront property in the heart of Santa Monica. "It's on sale for 3.5 million. You'd love this house, Mommy. I'll buy you one."

I cried of joy because of her beautiful thought. I didn't doubt her.

Amelia was attending UCLA. (That, too, I only found out long after she enrolled.) Casually over dinner, she told me that she would be in the Miss California contest. I asked, "When did you get into pageants?"

She said she was recruited and thought it would get her scholarships. Amelia wasn't the pageant type, and I never heard her talk of pageantry, let alone being in one.

I never told the girls about my experience with pageants.

The first one was in kindergarten, which certainly wasn't my idea. Dressed in a white satin gown, I was the first runner-up with a swollen face and red eyes. The second time was in high school. I was recruited. That pageant was in a different town, and the lady who was the head of an organization wanted me to represent them. The good thing was that most likely, nobody knew me, so if I sucked, no one would care. Besides, it was a last-minute thing, leaving little time to prepare. I didn't have a budget for clothing, and the makeup was so heavy that I looked like some befallen Greek deity cursed by Dionysus. I didn't win, but again, I was the first runner-up for the million-dollar smile I put on. Someone told me I should have won the crown just for that. The next day I went to school and took a seat in the back, tardy from the late night. In the first class, my teacher announced that he had attended the pageant. I thought, *Oh dear God, please, no*. My teacher started talking more about the pageant and how he noticed that someone in his class was in the show. I shrunk in my seat. When he said my name, everyone turned around only to find me trying to hide under my desk.

Amelia had no idea that her being in the Miss California pageant was a big deal for me. I think I was more excited than her. Two weeks before the show, I was anxious to get her evening gown. Amelia, on the other hand, hadn't even thought of it. She was occupied with work and focused on the upcoming semester.

"Sweetie, we have to get your evening gown at least," I reminded her two weeks out.

"Oh, I'll get to it as soon as I get a chance," she replied calmly.

A week before the event, still no evening gown.

On the first day of rehearsal, as soon as Amelia arrived at the venue in Palm Springs, she took a photo of her name tag. She had taken *my* last name. Initially, she and Asia had Harvey's last name. Then Drake's mother decided the girls should have Drake's last name. When we moved to L.A., the girls decided to change their last names to Prem legally. So, on this first rehearsal, her name tag read Amelia Prem. She thought it would mean so much to me, and it did. I broke down and cried. I wouldn't miss making a hotel reservation in Palm Springs to attend the Miss California pageant!

Just three days away, I became more concerned that Amelia didn't have an evening gown. Why was I stressing? I wasn't the one in the pageant. But I was relieved when Amelia called and said, "I got my evening gown. It's beautiful, elegant, and deep, rich aubergine."

When Amelia sent pictures, it was so gorgeous that I was afraid to ask about the cost.

"Oh my God, it's perfect! How much?"

"It's practically new. Fits me perfectly. And it was on sale for four dollars," she told me.

For some reason, I thought she was shopping at Saks Fifth Avenue in Beverly Hills. "What? Saks has it on sale for four dollars? That's insane. That must be a mistake."

"Oh no, I'm at Goodwill. Yeah, four dollars," she reassured me.

My mind went to a scene on the red carpet where the interviewer asks, "Amelia, who are you wearing?" And she replies, "Goodwill." But in reality, that filled me with tremendous joy, to know that my daughter is amazingly different. I was beyond proud of her. Ultimately, Amelia didn't compete. She bowed out to accept a real estate management position instead. I needed to go to therapy just from her withdrawing from the pageant!

◇◇◇◇◇◇◇◇◇◇◇◇

Amelia had always kept things to herself and made important decisions on her own. I remember how the first couple of weeks in high school, she often came home depressed. When I asked her what was wrong, she confessed, "They don't wear backpacks, they carry Louis Vuitton, drive BMWs or Benzes."

I sat next to her, wondering what I could say to drain the negativity out of her system. Amelia was carrying a load that I couldn't take from her and carry, which hurt.

We heard that their grandmother Mildred, Harvey's mother, was seriously ill in the hospital in San Francisco. Amelia found out through their grandfather Donald, Harvey's dad. Amelia stayed in touch with him, primarily through email. We had visited Donald and Mildred a couple of times when Amelia was about seventeen. Amelia suggested that we go to see Mildred. "I have a feeling that's going to be the last time we see her."

It would also be one of the very few times they'd seen her. The girls were Mildred's only granddaughters, but they'd seen each other no more than five times in their entire lives.

My heart melted when Amelia told me about Mildred. Here's a teenager who cared greatly about a grandmother who was never around. She could have done other teenage things. But she wanted to drive up to San Francisco to pay one last visit to her grandma, who never once changed a diaper. I couldn't miss work, so I told the girls they could go without me. It would be their first time on the road driving from Los Angeles to San Francisco, but they promised to check in with me along the way.

They reached San Francisco without incident and headed straight to see their grandma in the hospital. I can only imagine her expression when she saw the faces of two angels. Although she hadn't been around Amelia and Asia, they made the effort to be there for her. Her life was probably extended just a little longer, giving her enough time to review what she coulda, woulda, and shoulda done with them.

Of course, my girls ran into Harvey. That visit would not have been complete without him in the picture. That night in their hotel, they called me. Whatever Asia saw in Harvey that day gave her a strong impression. "I don't see how I could be related to this man." Then, she summed it up in one succinct line: "I could have sworn I was born from an egg to an egg."

"I'm really glad you left when you did," Amelia said with an incredibly soothing voice that reverberated in my soul as the ultimate seal that I had done the best thing for us. She saw how she might have turned out—a beaten-up, empty soul, devoid of life and dependent on bottled spirits just to get through the day.

A couple of months later, in 2010, all three of us drove up to the Bay Area to pay our respects to their late grandmother. On our drive up, I looked forward to seeing Harvey. I imagined being in the final championship round in the boxing ring with him. When we arrived at Harvey's place, I thought there would be a gathering of mourners, where Harvey would deliver a tear-jerking eulogy that just breaks my heart so badly I would want to throw myself at him out of pity. Instead, Harvey took us straight to his garage, cluttered with random items collected over the years. He showed us an old Cadillac limousine that was probably costing him more to store than it was worth and what he claimed was the first Apple computer. We hadn't made the trip to see his shit. We went there to pay our respects to his mother. There was no gathering. No eulogy. And nobody there other than us. His mother was confined to a tin coffee can, and a rusty one at that! I glanced at Amelia and Asia with the expression, *Am I the only one seeing this shit?* I wasn't; they had the same face. I shook my head, thinking, *We drove all the way here for this!*

Harvey, in tears, suddenly handed me a handwritten note from his mother, stating that three of her cars be given to me. The note broke his heart because he thought they should have been his. Bless her soul. I accepted the generous gesture. She knew that we needed a car, and she left me *three*. The only issue was that none of them worked, and they weren't safe enough to sit in. I wasn't about to fight over that little note. I suggested splitting the money if he took the cars to the junkyard.

Then out of nowhere, Harvey did the most embarrassing thing in front of my daughters. He got down on his knees, trying to woo me by telling them how beautiful their mother was. Good Lord! That did nothing for me, but the thing that impressed me was how Amelia and Asia treated him. They showed him respect—as a human being. Nothing more. Nothing less. They definitely didn't see Harvey as their father. Although he hadn't done anything for them and never became the man he could have been, they respected him. I was proud of them for that.

As we were leaving, Harvey asked if we could drop him off somewhere. It was pouring rain when Amelia pulled alongside the curb at an intersection and her father hopped out. She got out of the car to tell him goodbye and handed him an umbrella. The sight of that simple gesture melted my heart. "Amelia and Asia are more than alright," I mumbled as tears rolled down my cheeks, fogging up my glasses.

11.

T. Rex Encounter

A T THE TIME, I WAS STUDYING THEATER. I WAS AT home rehearsing with Marco, an Armani-model type of European descent. We met at an actor and director lab and were working on a play by Federico García Lorca called *Blood Wedding*. We worked well together. Marco was about to leave when the girls came home with a serious somebody-is-in-trouble look on their faces. *My God*, I thought. *What have I done?*

"We need to talk," Amelia insisted. She was fighting to hold back tears. I'd *never* seen her like that. Asia was standing next to her sobbing. My stomach knotted as I ushered Marco out the door, thinking of the time the girls sat me down and told me I couldn't date.

Before they dove too far into their thought process, I blurted out, "Is it Marco? Marco's gay!" When their expressions didn't change I realized something else was going on and my mind went to—somebody's pregnant. "What is it?" I insisted. "What's wrong?"

Amelia trembled with rage as she spoke. "It's about Drake." Asia sobbed harder as her sister prepared to drop the bomb on me. "Drake is a sick person! He did it to me! And he did it to Asia too!"

A vicious dinosaur took a bite of my insides, piece by piece, chewed my organs, and left my heart bleeding while sucking every ounce of oxygen out of me. My brain shut down in a massive blackout. My whole life, I had tried to prevent sexual abuse from happening to my children, but I failed miserably. I had a deep resentment toward my mother for not protecting me, yet I hadn't protected my girls. Both of them. How could I have missed it? I was sucked inside a black hole where something malfunctioned, causing it to collapse with me inside.

As a raging force physically overcame me, I tried gaining some semblance of strength. I reached for my phone to call Drake's mother. But Amelia stopped me.

"We want you out of this. This—is our fight."

Still crying in incredible pain, Asia added, "We want to press charges!"

I took the girls to the local police station to file the report. Amelia and Asia insisted I wait outside. They didn't want me to hear the sickening and maddening details. I waited, and a torturous mental and emotional death overcame me.

◇◇◇◇◇◇◇◇◇◇◇

Drake was in Hawaii for the initial investigation with the police, and he told them he needed time to get a lawyer. They gave it to him, and, of course, Drake fled the country. My seventeen- and nineteen-year-old girls were told he was traveling all over Asia with his mother's financial support. The last we heard, he was couch-surfing in India. My girls made a deliberate decision to move on with their lives and do therapy. The stress of wondering about his whereabouts was simply too painful. With every move Drake made, it was like yanking off a scab. The three of us shifted our focus to our healing.

There was this T. rex that was killing me, and the feeling took me back to my profound grief. It was no longer about the fact that my relatives had molested me. I had to come to terms with that. My grief was so intense because my heart felt bound with a rusty chain. I had failed my daughters. I resented my mother so deeply, yet I couldn't protect my own daughters. I did worse to my daughters, but they were still supportive, loving, and utterly forgiving.

I told my girls that it's not what happened but what we do that will define us. Faith in those words restored hope and opened me to new and expansive possibilities. The sexual abuse that happened to both my daughters hurled me to a bottomless pit of despair, crying from my soul, where I was left to begin my healing.

I didn't excuse Drake for the sinful things he'd done. Yet I held myself fully accountable for what happened. I believed that deep down, on a subconscious level, I must have harbored a negative vibration that allowed the horrible experience to occur. That was something that I needed to change. I needed to uproot the negativity from my psyche. Wherever it came from, it had to end with me. So I found myself tracking the root to the beginning—the very beginning.

Shit happens, but I don't have to live and smell like it. Life made sure that I understood this fundamental shit principle. There is always a choice, and it can be made only with conscious effort. The power lies in the degree of consciousness we put into the process. The outcome can be cathartic.

I was young and void of answers or solutions, so my trauma contributed to my running away. I thought if I just went far enough away, over the mountain ridges, that shit would disappear. Poof! But it didn't. The shit followed me like a shadow. That was the best thing I knew. It began when I was in third grade and followed me until sophomore year in high school. I didn't know how to heal or combat it. That was my level of consciousness, so I had to start where I was—that's all I could do.

I was fooling myself and simply avoiding the issues because there's no such thing as running away. I thought it would give me a chance to rebuild, reconstruct the broken system, and rewire my brain and trace all synapses that needed reconnecting. The more conscious my choices, the more synapses reconnect. How do I know I'm making conscious choices? Conscious choices meant that my whole being was involved. The body, mind, heart, and soul are all in; the entire team is on one page, as opposed to your mind wanting something, your heart wanting something else, the poor body getting the brunt in the form of disease, and the soul wanting nothing to do with that shit.

I came to understand my trauma as it relates to my daughters' trauma. In that vantage point, forgiving myself and others came naturally. Blaming or pointing fingers is futile, while forgiving is logical. In addition to her three jobs and school load, Amelia attended a support therapy group. I dove deeper into meditation, yoga, and breath work to speed up my healing process so I could help Asia, who struggled with posttraumatic stress disorder. Asia was attending San Francisco State University at the height of her PTSD. When she had panic attacks, I was on the phone listening, and it was painful. Indescribably painful.

Sometimes she'd run out of the class when triggers hit. Crying as she fled across campus, trying to contain the monstrous anxiety possessing her nervous system as she made her way to the nurse's clinic—I was still holding the phone. Asia was sitting in the clinic holding the pills they offered to calm her, insisting, "I don't want to take antidepressants. I don't want my life to be dependent on these pills."

"Then don't," I replied, mirroring her conviction. I told Asia, "Right now, your health, your mental and emotional health, are most important. Schools are not going anywhere. There are as many schools on this planet as there are Starbucks on every corner. And these schools will be there if you decide to leave and go back fifty years later. Take a break and focus on your health."

At first, she thought I was just trying to cheer her up. But Asia had an unyielding will to muscle through that debilitating condition in her most vulnerable, fragile state. When she held those pills in her hand while in the height of posttraumatic triggers and still had the presence of mind to recognize that she was better off without them, she displayed her strong will, and it needed to be nurtured.

12.

Here I Am!

AMELIA DOESN'T TALK ABOUT THINGS. SHE JUST does them, like her engagement—no big deal. I just saw a ring with diamonds all around it on her right ring finger. Although I didn't know for sure, I figured it was an engagement ring. My perception of the matter seemed blurry. Trying to be respectful, I didn't make a big deal of it.

"That's a nice ring," I said, trying to contain myself.

"Yeah, thank you" was all she said.

After Amelia's graduation in 2013, I drove her and her fiancé to LAX since they were heading to Australia. By then, I had processed the significant change she was making. I was happy to see her spread her wings as I had done, but I was a bit worried. After taking their luggage out of my trunk, we hugged goodbye. Suddenly Amelia broke into sobs. The weight lifted off my chest, and with a long sigh, I said, "You're gonna be okay, kiddo. You're gonna have fun discovering life."

When they walked into the airport, my eyes filled with tears, but I was happy to watch her go live her life. I loved seeing her taking risks, venturing out, and exploring different ways of life other than the American way. Amelia would live her life the way she wanted, not how others or even I saw it. The beautiful thing is that she could gracefully change her mind at any point. It was a joy to see her in pursuit of life, thoughtfully making decisions even when faced with uncertainty—without interference to her process. I found it a tremendous favor to myself and others to relinquish control.

<><><><><><><><><>

My mother came to America for the first time in 2013. I wished Papa could have come with her, but death got to him first. Nowadays, he comes a lot more often. It's much easier traveling internationally when you're not bogged down by any physical restrictions. But that's a whole different experience than coming to America on a Boeing jet plane.

Mama coming was a very exciting event. She was staying for at least six months, and I was curious to see how the reality of America compared to her idea of it. When I left our village all those years ago, I never dreamed of anything like this. I wasn't sure I was prepared for what Mama might think. I was also anxious about church. I hadn't been to Catholic Church since I came to America, but going to church every day was Mama's primary activity, so I scoped out a couple of churches she could walk to.

Mama took a direct flight from Manila to LAX. It was her first time on a big plane. She was experiencing a smidgen of what I went through. Mama doesn't have a cell phone. She lives in a village with no phones, but that's fine with her. She doesn't get technology. So I instructed her to go with the flow and follow where everybody is going because everyone would come out the same way. At the very end, you'll see people holding signs with names of the people they're picking up; that's where I'll be, looking for you.

Knowing it would take a while to get through immigration for first entry, I arrived an hour after her flight, but I didn't think I'd spend six freaking hours scanning every face that came through, but not hers. So when my phone rang, I was quick to answer the unknown local number.

"Hello? Hello, *Dejaaa*, it's your mother."

Mama has a way of saying my name like she's not quite sure because she is still in the process of accepting it as my new name.

"Mama, it's still me. The same person that came out of your birth canal."

She called me from Starbucks, not too far from where everybody comes out after customs. She asked the person at Starbucks if they wouldn't mind dialing my number, which she had handy. The Starbucks person called me from their cell. Mama spoke a few English words with a heavy accent; although, to make that phone call happen, she mostly used sign language. I was proud that she was proud of herself.

When I finally laid eyes on Mama, she looked so confident. Her chestnut eyes were lit with excitement as though she had conquered the world. Mama doesn't like accessories, no earrings or makeup, and no worries—she just had her big, beautiful smile. She had only one small shoulder bag that contained all her immigration documents. She didn't have to bother with baggage claim. Mama traveled the way I did, very light. Besides, we could just get whatever clothes she needed. We walked to my car, a pearl white hybrid Prius. When I opened the door for

162 DEJA VU PREM

Mama, and she climbed inside such a high-tech vehicle, I could tell she had a unique dimensional experience. My parents never owned a car. Our method of transportation was pretty much in the form of two feet, usually in flip-flops. For the first time, I drove Mama—and in new, modern vehicle. I knew it was blowing her mind. Inside the Prius, she could see the screen monitor showing the different working mechanisms as we slithered through the under- and overpass, intersecting the 405 freeway—the massive infrastructure of Los Angeles, which her brain calls "America." Everything hit her viscerally on top of the jet lag.

We were silent as we both processed. In her deep silence, I could feel her thought: *How the fuck did I make it here on my own?* Of course, she didn't know that versatile English word exists. Before we went to my place, I took her to a restaurant on the Santa Monica promenade that served a hybrid of Asian foods. The waiter came to take our order, and Mama looked confused. She'd never been waited on. This made her kind of uncomfortable, but she didn't say anything. The food arrived and we ate. When the bill came, she asked how much it costs. I told her the dinner was about sixty-five dollars plus a tip. It upset her to hear the dollar amount. In her mind, she could have made a much more palatable dinner for maybe five bucks, and she would have enjoyed serving it too.

When we got to my place, I observed Mama doing the same things she did for me back home, but somehow, I felt different watching her dive into work before enjoying her trip or time with me. While she was visiting, Mama washed my laundry by hand *every* day, my underwear in particular. And that was after showing her how to use the laundry machines. Mama found them more cumbersome and costly. My apartment was spotless. She chased every dust particle out the window—just like back home.

For Ash Wednesday, we attended a mass at Saint Monica Church. While Mama got up and did all the rituals, I remained seated and noticed the worried look on her face. After service, Mama asked why I didn't do the ash. Triggered by her questioning and feeling judged, my whole body grew tense. I said to myself, *Okay, here we go. Don't react. She's the pope, you know. Breathe. Stay calm. She's not really judging you. She's just curious. Maybe she just wants to understand how you may have changed over the years. Okay.* After stealing a few moments to process her question and my response, I said, "Mama, I had a talk with God. There's way too much to remember: Good Friday, Ash Wednesday, Easter Sunday, and on and on with all the other days. I asked God to simplify it to maybe one or two things that I could remember every day, and remember well. God boiled it down to two things: love yourself, beyond narcissism, and love others, but not kissing ass. That I can remember even in my sleep."

Mama said, "I understand."

"Phew!" I said, sighing in relief.

After mass we went to the Self-Realization Fellowship Lake Shrine, founded by Paramahansa Yogananda, and attended a service and discourse by a monk. I was quite surprised by how receptive Mama was to the Eastern practice of meditation. The monk talked about how some things don't change, saying, "You can send a cat to the monastery, but the cat will not become a monk. It will still be a cat."

"That monk is quite a comedian," Mama joked.

One of her all-time favorite movies is *The Ten Commandments*, so I took her to Universal Studios. It was worth every penny of the season pass, which we only used that one day, to see Mama beyond amused when she saw how, using the magic of Hollywood practical effects, Moses parted the Red Sea. Mama was like a girl who finally met her childhood idol. I knew she couldn't wait to go home and tell everybody about it.

Growing up, Mama always woke us up at the crack of dawn

to recite the rosary. I thought the whole religious ritual was over-rated and not my thing. I just fucking wanted my sleep. Now in the comfort of my own nest, Mama still bugged me with the same ritual. Admittedly, it was nice to see Mama at peace doing her routine as soon as she woke up, and she did leave me to sleep during that time. Except I heard her mumbling her prayers, in particular the part where she recited the things she wanted. I noticed it was more than a religious ritual—I found it was how she gets through the day. If I hadn't disovered that, waking up at four would have been a lot to give up, especially since I couldn't go back to sleep. Eavesdropping, I discovered that her prayers were about me. *They were all about me.* When will that change? Everything was but a reflection of me. Mama kept praying for God to send the right man for me. Good Lord! After hearing that, I was so awake! What a tragic misfortune that I lost my dear husband. Now look at me, all alone. Maybe I just needed to take her to Disneyland. To be clear, I'm not complaining. Mama doted on me the same way she did my girls when I took them home. By the time I went off to bed, my breakfast was ready. My laundry was hand-washed and folded. She'd figured out how to operate the vacuum, even running it under my feet. Cobwebs were nowhere in sight and the dishes were sparkling clean on the dish rack. So many things were getting done while she was on her knees in prayer.

One morning at breakfast, Mama led with grace before the first bite. But then we never got to the first bite and the rest of the scrambled eggs. My mother went into a different litany that time. I should emphasize that my mother's recital of this partic-ular litany directed toward me was an agonizing reminder of this double-edged sword penetrated deep in my psyche, through no fault of my own. By who? No one in particular, but everyone was responsible. It's the passing of the torch through lineage. The torch is the pain and sorrows of the past, in billions of lifetimes. It sucks that I got myself involved in this ancestral business, but I consider myself lucky to be the one to break the cycle. I get to work my ass off so I can pass not pain and sorrow but heal from it, moving forward with grace, love, and joy.

Mama recited her litany in Latin. That ancient language seemed to naturally roll off her tongue like poetry. It was a litany of all the things I'd done for my family since running away. While struggling as a single mother, I scraped up enough money to pay for my three siblings' college tuitions: my sister, my older brother, and my youngest brother. They all finished college. My youngest brother was named after my father and always got away with murder. Without fail, he was the one person that got on my nerves *big time*. But seeing him grow into a man of substance touched my heart. I was afraid he would be one odd lawyer, but I was wrong. Before he even passed the bar exam, working under someone else's title, he took a case pro bono, appearing in court wearing flip-flops matching his simple, disadvantaged penniless client. The case's unusual nature took it to the Supreme Court, and my little brother won. That was his first case. That made every hard-earned penny I sent him worth a bar of gold.

Neither of my parents had a chance to attend college, and in the Philippines, it's tough to get a decent job without a college degree. Mama barely finished fifth grade. Papa made it to the first year of high school. After all my siblings got their degrees, I supported my nephews and niece through college as well. Shortly after Papa passed away, I found out his wildest dream was that all his kids would finish college. In his quiet heart, he wanted my brother to become the lawyer he wished he could have been.

I thought helping someone fulfill their dream would propel me closer to mine. Being a single mom, I thought of my sister and how ten times tougher life must have been for her. I often looked at a dollar bill and thought how much further it would go if I sent it to my sister. For as much as I needed a dollar, it would always be just a dollar. For Sissy, a dollar was equal to a hundred. I'd also send my sister books like *The Power of Positive Thinking* by Norman Vincent Peale. I imagined her reading it and the synapses in her brain lighting up like fireworks as she made sense of things. Then toward the last few chapters, when she flipped open the page, she'd find a hundred-dollar bill I managed to put aside for her.

In one of my visits back home, my sister picked me up at the airport and took me to her house. It was pretty decent, much better, bigger, and more complete than our childhood home had been, with walls, windows, and doors, and of course, the roof was more solid and better than what we ever had growing up. As I walked inside, she told me, "This is your house." I thought she was being kind, warm, and welcoming, and that she wanted me to feel at home by telling me that. But she meant it's my house because I paid for it. I played it cool, but my heart trembled, and I cried out loud, *in silence*. Finally, I'd done something right. It was a joy beyond fulfillment.

Then there was my parents' dilapidated house with a river running out back, so the house constantly got flooded. I had the house torn down and rebuilt from the ground up, with a levy and an elevated ground floor about three feet high. I studied a bit of architecture and designed the house for them myself. I enjoyed reading about different designs and perspectives. I especially wanted to have a high ceiling as it would make it feel more expansive. Mama lives there. My father passed away before I had a chance to build it, but I know he would have loved it solely because I had it made for them.

By the time Mama wrapped up her morning litany, our breakfast was ice cold. But I was thankful. Mama had cut through all the fears and reservations I'd harbored for years. She'd recognized me. The great veil that hid Deja lifted in dissolution.

"I thought about you all these years," Mama said. "And how you are making it on your own. I'm sorry I couldn't be there for you and the girls. I prayed day and night for your strength and guidance."

Hearing those words from my mother made my heart bleed. But as much as it hurt, it was more healing. The bleeding was the draining of the sorrow so the heart could be open once again. I would have gone to the ends of the world to win that recognition—and it could come only from Mama. *My mama.* Before accepting her recognition, I had to be humble enough to admit my deep longing for it. I contemplated whether I ever felt important enough to deserve it. Then, I was grinning as I thought, *Of course, I am. I am! I am!* Awareness of this kind broke the negative pattern, activating the latent power within that causes a shift to positive programming rather than negative, and it serves my highest purpose.

We are not in this alone. This life journey has been a continuum. The more expanded our field of view, the more we can understand our place in the bigger scheme of things. I'm doing myself and everyone before and after me a big favor by considering what is asked of me. How can I be a beacon of light in my path and for others? This involves recognizing what is no longer serving the highest good and upgrading what could be of service for the greater good. Raising my awareness is key to identifying what was passed on to me and how I move forward with clarity and purpose. The goal is not to repeat negative patterns from the previous generation but to break free from limiting beliefs.

In healing my trauma, I had simultaneous and tremendous healing in my relationship with my family. There was a reconnection with Mama that garnered trust and love. The outcome was that I no longer needed to seek it from anyone else. In forgiving myself, I've developed the capacity to forgive my mother and others who have caused me pain. Forgiving is letting go of the negative experience so we can move forward in the continuum instead of repeating the same destructive patterns. This helped me to see that I matter. I can make a difference. I am enough. I have always been enough. I am here to make a difference.

Before Mama returned to the Philippines, I decided to take her on a tour of the five-star hotel where I worked. I never told my family what I did for work to avoid explaining what it entailed and having it misconstrued, but it was time. I didn't want her to worry about how I earned the money I sent home. She'd never been to a five-star hotel, and it blew her brain. She didn't know what a day spa was until we went inside. As we ventured from one area to another, my colleagues greeted Mama by her name. When we entered the women's locker room, Mama saw other women naturally preparing to relax like it was part of their daily routine. This was the type of life Mama deserved but had never experienced.

"There's the shower, the steam room, and sauna," I said, pointing them out to her. "And here's your slippers and robe." I escorted Mama to the lounge area, where the massage therapist would pick her up for a two-hour indulgent massage. "And if you're lucky, you'll get the best one in the house." After an hour, she was all warm and toasty from lounging. The masseuse took exceptional care of her. Oh, Mama got the best—me! Of course, she wasn't surprised.

There was still a part of me that hadn't forgiven her for failing to protect me from sexual abuse, especially since it made me consider how my girls felt about me failing to do the same for them. It was a harrowing thought. If I forgave myself, and surely my daughters forgave me, I can forgive Mama. But perhaps, I hadn't forgiven Mama because I hadn't forgiven myself.

I drove Mama over to a mansion in Malibu, California, to see one of my favorite clients, Sophie, a philanthropist. She's a generous and thoughtful person. She would already have everything set up for me, so I'd show up with my best self every week, sometimes twice a week. Once when she was distraught over her mother's death, I went twenty minutes over because I felt she needed that extra time. She heard my mother was visiting and insisted that I bring her with me. Mama had never been in a house with three different gates.

When the massive iron door buzzed open, we stepped inside, and Mama's jaw dropped. Sophie showed Mama around her little hut, embarrassed and amused at the same time— embarrassed because she thought her house was a closet compared to some others, amused because she was desensitized to how she lived. My mother's astonishment reminded her what a lucky bitch she was. Sophie started a movie in her entertainment room, and prepared some buttery popcorn for Mama while I did the massage. I knew Mama was bored; it was too much for her—talk about culture shock.

As soon as we left Sophie's and got in my car, I showed Mama the check I received every time I massaged Sophie. Mama's eyes bugged out when she saw the amount. All she had known were people who worked hard and lived off crumbs. I made $400 for a two-hour session plus $100 for every ten minutes I went over. In the Philippines, that amounted to someone's professional salary for a month working like a dog. With the money, I took Mama shopping for shoes, clothes, and anything she liked. She had never shopped like that before. I just wanted her to experience going to the store and getting whatever she loved for its quality,

design, and function. I wanted to show her that this is why I
went over the mountain ridges to the land of milk and honey—
opportunity. I had adversities. I learned from them and worked
to grow out of them. I had goals that I achieved and a vision that
I executed without a playbook. I found love lived inside of me
when I felt the love I had for my daughters. I wanted Mama to
see that this was my place of growth and healing. Every waking
moment I spent daydreaming about going over the mountain
ridges was worth it, as every waking moment of life matters.

Mama wanted to take home a couple of bags of roasted al-
monds, some chocolates to give away, and six big packages of
Himalayan pink salt. I got her a couple of nice, light, hard-shell
suitcases in bright orange so she wouldn't have to look for her
luggage; when she went to baggage claim, it would scream at
her. Mama was all packed for her flight, and she spotted some
of my dirty laundry from the last day, and again, she started
hand-washing it.

"Just leave them," I told her. "Why don't you take a bath
while I get the table set up for your massage?" By then, Mama
had learned to do what I said without my twisting her arm. For
two hours, she zoned out and went to heaven. It dawned on
me that my life was never held back by the love I didn't get as a
child. A whole world was unfolding before me simply with the
love I was now giving.

I took Mama to a nice Asian restaurant for dinner before
her flight. This time, Mama was much more present and really
seemed to enjoy dinner and allow herself to be served. It was a
Zen, sacred dinner with Mama that would not be the first or the
last time. The filled silence gave me a sense of profound connect-
edness, and we had the best conversation—a kind of boundless
communion.

At the airport, I walked Mama to the security check area

and hugged her the way I wanted her to hug me when I was a little girl. Mama hugged me back the same way. Then, as we let go to part ways, Mama cried.

I said, "Mama, you got this. Remember to go with the flow. If you're not sure, just ask. And you know who to ask. The right person, Mama. I know this sounds incredibly specific, but I will wait here until the flight takes off. And trust that you got on it with your seat belt buckled up." Seat belts are one of the things she learned about in America. It was hard watching Mama leave because that time brought us closer together.

Back home, I stared at myself in the bathroom mirror. After all that transpired with Mama, I couldn't think of anything to do but shave my head. First thing after shaving my head, I went over to Asia's home to have lunch with her. Ironically, we saw each other more often than when we lived together.

"Are you having a midlife crisis?" Asia asked, carefully observing my head.

"I always wanted to shave my head like a monk," I replied.

"That's what people do when they go through a midlife crisis, they shave their heads," she reassured me.

My intrinsic good looks are not up for argument. "Don't I look holy?" I asked suggestively.

"It's hot. I love it," she admitted.

I took a selfie and sent it to Amelia to see what other kind of approval I could get, and she sent the quickest reply I've ever gotten. "That's intense, man," she texted back.

"Yes!" I shouted, and punched the air. I just got into the most exclusive club. That meant a lot to me. There's an air of total openness out of respect and unconditional love. *Go on. Be yourself. I love you always.* It's out of this world.

◇◇◇◇◇◇◇◇◇

The whole leaving home thing was contagious. Asia decided she needed to get her own place to honor her sense of independence. The two sisters must have had a United Nations kind of convention about moving on, being grown-ups, and being on their own. For all those years, my identity revolved around being a single mother, and that identity was ripped from me, except I was still single and still a mother. I felt the empty-nest syndrome. After the girls were gone, my attraction to women grew stronger. I still hadn't dealt with the unresolved feelings. I got a lot of pressure from my colleagues to get out and start meeting people to increase my chances of finding that right person. But instead, I thought I needed to improve my breathing skills, so I started with all kinds of yoga to make up for all the dating I missed.

When I came to America, I had Taylor's phone number, but Harvey took my phone book. Over the years, Taylor and I had spoken a couple of times, but we'd lost touch. I remembered her father's name, so I looked him up. He told me his daughter lived in Colorado and was a resort manager up in Vail. He gave me her number and I left Taylor a message. When she called me back—I froze. My voice cracked when I spoke to her, and she didn't sound any better. I felt my rapid heartbeat pulsating in my throat and was at a loss for words. She could probably tell that I was freaking out. Besides, her questions weren't helping.

"Are you happy?" she asked. I thought, *Fuck, start with something softer.* Start from zero! My nerves were out of control and I didn't respond. She broke the silence and asked, "Are you okay?"

"Yeah, I'm okay."

"I looked for you."

"You couldn't have found me. I changed my name."

She gasped.

I told her about my daughters, and she told me about her children, who were five and seven years old.

She said, "My daughter's name is Lucia." I fell silent. Taylor named her after me. She said, "I still have that portrait."

I didn't know how to take it or what to say. Then Taylor said something that freaked me out. My nerves were combusting. "You know I pass by L.A. driving to San Diego, and we should hook up."

When we got off the phone, I deleted her number. I didn't know how to process the conversation and convinced myself that we weren't meant to be.

As a child, I saw that the mindset of everyone in my village was fairly limited in scope. Instinctively, I opposed that mindset. I believed that there had to be more, which challenged me to expand my heart and soul. This is life; we are supposed to continue to grow. We can't see the edges of the Universe because there are no borders, so there is no end to this expansion.

I had just finished a three-year program in intensive screenwriting in which half the time I spent pulling my hair to get out of my logical mind and into the conceptual and the intuitive side of the right brain. It was the reward I'd given myself for sending a good portion of my money to help my family in the Philippines. After working my ass off, I was pleased to have done something for myself, but now that it was over, I found myself alone and without distraction.

With my girls gone, I decided to move rather than pay twenty-five hundred a month to live alone. I rented a private room and private bath in a house with others I could interact with. Maybe it was the empty-nest syndrome. I felt a deep need to nurture and mother, but I didn't realize that I needed nurturing and mothering myself. I felt a deep pain in my soul—longing for meaningful existence.

I sat down, wondering what would happen if I meditated three hours in the morning and two hours in the evening for three months. That's five hours I'd miss doing things. I'd been running around like a chicken with its head cut off. What could I be missing? I decided that three months was nothing compared to a lifetime in Zombieland—so I began.

The moment I closed my eyes, the war began. Thoughts fighting other thoughts, body parts itching one after another, and random thoughts coming. I parked on the wrong side of the street, the parking police wrote a ticket and left it under my windshield wiper, and blah blah blah. Soon enough, those thoughts lost their power over me as I realized they had no inherent significance but to strengthen my resolve. They were the gatekeeper to the sacred temple of silence. There lies the understanding of my suffering and its cessation, the sweet nectar of loving peace. I would have taken a limousine, but that path to silence was so treacherous it could be accessed only by foot.

While on a hike, I'd burst into a growling cry for no apparent reason. My heart wrung out every ounce of sorrow. It burned as it cracked open after all these years, and the hurt was so great. That unusual purge arrived on time every day for six months during meditation, whether on a hike or sitting still. I couldn't go about my day without meditation, yet I felt I had more time in the day. That time wasn't to run around doing things but to slow down, smell the roses along the way, and savor the subtle, flavorful sip of hot water. It seemed that time had lent itself bending backward and forward to accommodate life's necessities.

◇◇◇◇◇◇◇◇◇◇◇◇

I heard of this amazing retreat place in Big Sur with gourmet food, which they grew. I'd been working like a dog and needed to unplug. If I didn't find a way to give to myself, there would be a massive revolt taking place as an eruption inside me.

Driving up the winding coastal road along high cliffs to Big Sur in 2014, slivers of sunlight cut through the fog, creating a kind of mystical, altered reality; the sight of it hit me like a brick behind the wheel. I burst into tears, sobbing profusely for no reason. Not that I was aware of it, but I must have been holding it in. I really should have pulled over, yet I couldn't stop. It felt good to keep going and let myself go at the same time. I permitted myself to feel the way I needed at that moment. I blasted the radio while screaming at the top of my lungs. Eventually, I pulled over by this lookout on the cliff. Coming from the metropolitan noise of Los Angeles to the deafening silence of nature in that steep ravine, about a six-hour drive, I couldn't help but notice a crossing of a chasm between distinctive realities. Silence can be deafening. It's through silence that I'm able to hear the distractive noise bombarding my senses, cutting me off from the source, *the truth*. So I took refuge in silence.

I checked myself into that little piece of heaven nestled on a cliff's edge, suspended a hundred feet above the crashing surf and kelp-congested tides of the Pacific Ocean. With the guardhouse behind me, I realized there was no turning back. The first seven days at the retreat were an intense dose of painful silence that I wasn't accustomed to in Los Angeles. It would take at least two weeks just to recalibrate my brain. I signed up for a couple of workshops, one of which was intimacy. Deep, meaningful intimacy. The workshop consisted mainly of young couples. It was painful to watch some of them making such a tremendous effort to get into it. Maybe I was just perturbed because I was there with no one.

That intimacy workshop got me all worked up and ready for a deeper unplugging. The host for the next workshop stood in the middle of a campfire circle surrounded by about thirty people, all of whom were curious or in search of an alternative way to cope with this elusive reality called the modern world. He was getting ready to breathe out fire like a dragon. His name was John Perkins, and he wrote *Confessions of an Economic Hit Man.* In his book, he explains that his job, as he was told by his superior, was "to encourage world leaders to become part of a vast network that promotes U.S. commercial interests. In the end, those leaders become ensnared in a web of debt that ensures their loyalty. We can draw on them whenever we desire—to satisfy our political, economic, or military needs. In turn, they bolster their political positions by bringing industrial parks, power plants, and airports to their people. The owners of U.S. engineering and construction companies become fabulously wealthy."

One day as the shit hit the fan for John, he realized the implications of selling his soul. During the plan to undermine the rainforest to drill more oil, he met shamans from indigenous tribes who enlightened him of the devastations he and whatever clowns he was working for were causing. Horrified by the global scale of mass destruction weighing on his conscience, he quit being an economic hit man and became a shaman. He aspired to educate people and integrate a way of life that's sustainable in alignment with nature.

Until I met John, I never talked about the haunting thoughts of my grandfather, a shaman, and a hard-core one. He wore only a loincloth while traveling into other dimensions riding a flying dragon. The thought of following my grandfather's footsteps contributed to my running away, fearing that I would be confined to an old-fashioned way of life otherwise. And to imagine myself wearing just a loincloth. Such a limiting choice of wardrobe. What about America? John helped me understand how I could be of service in integrating shamanism in the modern world. Ignorance is not bliss. Enlightenment is. John was a hit man leading a shamanism retreat, and that retreat helped me connect to my grandfather as a shaman. The very thing that has given me the imagination to fly and transcend life, and the tools to break out of the limiting mold and suffocating conformity, was Grandfather.

I was given a precious gift of life, and it is not solely for me. The gift is for everyone. But to see, understand, and have gratitude for it, I needed to experience the world for its glory and suffering. The trick is not to get caught up in either one but to rise above its dual nature to transcend. I guess God must have been bored to come up with this game, though I prefer to call it the play of life, with everyone starring as the lead. For sure, I'm the lead in my own epic. Let me play it big. I don't want to bore the Universe.

In truth, God has no name. You can refer to it in only so many ways. At first, you become miserable, freak out, and get bent out of shape when shit happens. But as you gain wisdom and hopefully crack your heart open—because it is only ultimately with an open heart that you can see what the freaking gift really is—when you're finally open enough to see it, you'll laugh your ass off as your mind gets blown away by the ecstatic moment-to-moment occurrence. You are then living the gift. It's the ginormous four-letter word you've heard all over the place but only remotely understood. It's LOVE. This is what I was beginning to understand. I say *only beginning* because it is as vast as the Universe. It *is* the Universe, ever-expanding in its uncontainable infinite nature.

◇◇◇◇◇◇◇◇◇◇◇

By 2016, I was *still* gripping my secret, fighting self-acceptance, rejecting self-love, and fearing I would not have the acceptance of my family if they knew my secret. Lying in bed in a pitch-black room, a warm breeze filtered through the window, sweeping gently across my face. I was wide awake, contemplating removing fear, ready to live out loud. It was 2:00 a.m. in L.A. when I reached over to my night table and grabbed my phone. I took a deep breath and called my sister. It was 6:00 p.m. in the Philippines. Sissy taught English at the school, but I thought she'd be home.

When she answered in our Bisaya dialect, she said, "What is it?"

I took another deep breath to calm myself. Sharing myself and feeling vulnerable was new for me.

"Is everything okay?" she questioned, sounding worried.

My heart pounded against my chest. I told myself, *You just need to say it! Get over it!* We weren't face to face, and she couldn't beat me up even if she wanted to.

"I just wanted to tell you I'm gay."

Her immediate response was "Oh, that means you're happy."

Then I realized that was her English translation. I thought to myself, *Well, that didn't quite land, but all that matters is that I said it,* so I got off the phone. I turned over and placed my phone back on the nightstand, feeling a lack of accomplishment. I couldn't sleep. I said it, but since it didn't land, it didn't count.

The next day at the same time, I called my sister again. This time I wanted to make sure she understood me. If I wanted to love myself unconditionally, this was the time to prove it.

As soon as she answered, I said, "Everything's fine. But I really need for you to hear me. So, buckle up. Remember, we don't talk about awkward things—so this isn't easy." She was quiet, letting me know she was ready to hear me. *"I'm gay,"* I said, without rushing to get through it. I took a moment to let it land, and I could feel her taking it in. Then for clarity, I added, "Not 'gay' as in happy, but 'gay' as in I'm going to be with a woman. So, you have to stop praying that I'll find a husband because I don't want one! I didn't tell you before because I hadn't realized how

I really felt about it. And I had nothing to show for it—I still don't." Sissy was still very quiet, but I felt she heard me all the way. And just from her listening—I felt so much love. For the first time, I believed I'd finally given her a chance to love me—to love me as I am.

Sissy admitted, "We always thought something was different about you." She said it sweetly and without judgment. "I love you, sis. I'll always love you. I just want you to be happy with whoever you want to be with."

Hearing that acceptance from my sister filled my heart. She was the one I felt the closest to. After that conversation, I said to myself, *I'm good. I don't have to tell everyone. I don't think I have to tell Mama. Maybe that's not necessary. Not to mention it would be awkward. I'm good for now.*

Asia was twenty-two years old when I told her that I came out to Sissy, and she replied, "That's good. I wouldn't want anything to do with anybody who doesn't accept that about you."

Emboldened by her statement, I thought, *That's how accepting you should be of yourself.* Such a statement overwhelmed me with love. It reverberated in my consciousness. Humbled to be her *mother*, I found myself unable to speak, so I wrapped my arms around her.

Within that week, Sissy had told everybody! My family, including Mama, got on Viber, which is the communication platform we use in the Philippines. Everyone was kind of solemn but nice. Then Mama spoke up: "You look very handsome." I think they thought I had switched or changed from being a woman to a man. My sister said, "I love you, and you'll always be a girl to me."

I responded, "I didn't change my sex. But there are different shades to this."

I wanted to tell them, *I love this body. I love that I have a vagina!*

◇◇◇◇◇◇◇◇◇◇◇

Amelia called and asked if I wanted to go to Paris for a wedding—*hers*. Of course, I wouldn't miss it for the world. I asked to take those days off work, but my boss at the spa wouldn't let me go unless all my shifts were covered. At the same time, everyone at work wanted to take off, so there weren't enough subs to cover my shifts. So I quit. I worked at that place for eight years, but I wasn't going to miss my daughter's wedding.

Amelia had arranged my itinerary round-trip from L.A. to Paris. Unfortunately, Asia was in the middle of finals and couldn't attend. When I landed, Amelia had a driver pick me up from the airport and take me to a château several hours away where the wedding would be held. We picked up her fiancé's parents on the way. When the three of us arrived at the château, we were greeted by a staff of five. One gave us a tour of the château. It was filled with taxidermy, and I think it scared Amelia's future mother-in-law. After the tour, they decided to stay at a nearby hotel. I didn't blame them. The château felt haunted.

My heart was racing as we walked down the long spooky corridors where stuffed lions or tigers lurked around the corner. Here and there, I caught a glimpse of another safari creature winking at me. As we entered a massive room with a Marie Antoinette four-poster bed, my imagination ran rampant. The tour staff announced, "This is the bride's mother's bedroom," while I stood quietly behind him taking everything in. It was quite beautiful, but all I could think was that I hoped the château wasn't haunted. It would take me a good ten to fifteen minutes to run to the opposite wing, to Amelia's room.

I couldn't sleep that night because I wanted to experience every square inch of the glamorous antiquated atmosphere. I thought of all the festivities, the secret love affairs, and the masquerade balls, which were probably wilder in my vivid imagination. It was getting late, but the night was young when my mind grew bored with those useless thoughts. I decided to meditate until near dawn.

After a gourmet breakfast, the makeup artist arrived from Paris. She was part of the whole package deal. She had to only do me and Amelia, which felt very special. Everything Amelia arranged exceeded my expectations, and I felt incredibly honored to be her mother.

"Are you going to cry?" the makeup artist asked while curling my lashes.

"I don't think so. Wasn't planning on crying. That would mess up the mascara you're working on arduously. I'll smile, laugh, or do both instead."

Then came the heart-wrenching, memorable part where I walked my daughter down the aisle. I was super careful not to trip on Amelia's train. The groom's mother told me I was doing it wrong. I wondered, *How could you go wrong walking the bride down the aisle?* Then I discovered that, as it turned out, the bride was walking me. Well, that was the way Amelia and I usually walked down the street. I was always the one hanging onto her. No biggie. I knew I'd done something right.

After the wedding, I felt compelled to visit the sanctuary of Our Lady of Lourdes, which was about seven hours away. This site is renowned for the Marian apparitions claimed to have been seen by a peasant girl, Bernadette Soubirous, who was later canonized. I didn't know how to get to Lourdes, and I knew only a couple of words in French. One of which was my first name. But that didn't matter; a voice in my mind insisted that I had to be in Lourdes.

"Sweetie," I said to Amelia, "do you mind if I hop on a train to Lourdes right after the wedding?" I figured I would be doing

Amelia a favor by giving her and her new husband time to themselves for the honeymoon.

The irony was that now everybody wanted to go to Lourdes, so the honeymoon got rerouted. I didn't have to figure out how to read any French map because the honeymooners rented a van and drove to Lourdes. The only thing was that I wanted to experience this pilgrimage alone.

Well, I wasn't going to apologize for being selfish. I was under the influence of the bossy bitch voice in my head, but I didn't complain. I enjoyed being bossed around that way. I stayed five days alone in a foreign country without speaking a word of their language, which was equivalent to being in a silent retreat. May 13, 2017, turned out to be the centennial of the Virgin Mary apparitions. There were thousands of people from around the world participating in a massive procession, chanting "Ave Maria" while carrying lit candles. Being a speck in that mass, the consciously unifying event made my heart open; I felt elevated to an extraordinary height as my knees hit the ground. Something was happening to me. I had never felt so humbled that I dropped to my knees to kiss the ground in reverence to the divine intelligence orchestrating the Universe in which I am a dust particle. Every day I was in Lourdes, I drank and bathed in the holy water, which was a big deal. I found the biggest candle I could carry at the souvenir market, about four feet tall and seven inches in diameter. They have a special place for candles like that. When I lit my giant candle, I said a prayer requesting that *love* possess me in all its glory. I emphasized that I didn't know what love looked like—I didn't have the vaguest clue. And I added, "I leave the details to you. Surprise me."

After asking for my true love, in the middle of the special prayer of petition, I heard a voice say, "My precious child, I already did."

"Oh my God! Please unblind me. I want nothing but to be able to see your way."

While on my knees, overwhelmed with humility, I prayed, "I'm here. What do you want me to do? Stations of the Cross? I'll do that."

I wanted to make an offering of some significance. I was bestowing my quiet surrender and willingness to do what the voice said.

"Girl," the voice said. "Your whole life was the station of the cross. Go shopping."

The voice *never* ceased to surprise me. I wondered if I was merely having a crazy conversation with my insane self, and yet I went shopping. The bitch won, of course. Not Rodeo Drive shopping, just a couple of hand-carved souvenirs and an elegant rose-gold watch I'd always wanted. A watch like that in a pilgrimage site has got to be timeless.

From the rooftop of the ten-story hotel building I stayed in, I saw the region's tallest peak and decided to climb it the next day. The following morning, I caught a taxi and told the driver to take me to the foot of that peak. Most people don't hike to the top because it's dangerous, so I had to make my own path. I found it was an extreme course for downhill mountain biking when cyclists came flying down from nowhere. But luckily they were quite skilled and avoided me. Eventually, I made it to the top, where they had a couple of benches. I occupied one for about forty-five minutes. I could see the entire region surrounding Lourdes. Being there felt like a miracle. I sat there feeling strange for having climbed the peak but was okay with it—as that was my offering.

On the eleven-hour flight back to Los Angeles, two hours of turbulence felt like the aircraft wings would fall off. Oddly, I felt okay with it and prayed that it would be quick if it came down to it. Something had changed in me at the molecular level in Lourdes. I used to find it impossible even to doze off on flights, but despite the turbulence I fell fast asleep.

I had an old, quiet, obsessive fear that I wouldn't amount to the kind of filmmaker I wanted to be, one who created a significant body of work, and that I sacrificed myself and my daughters for *nothing*. That fear diminished during those two hours of turbulence and for the first time, I felt at peace. It's not that I'd given up on being a filmmaker. The passion has always been there. It's still there. What disappeared was the pressure that I had to make something or be somebody, the sponsoring thought that drives the belief of not being enough. With that clearance, I wanted to create something that resonated from the soul. Doing what you love will pay bills, but forget about paying the bills. Just love what you do, and honor that love. That will do so much more.

I have a great appreciation for the challenges I've grown through, as they've helped me hone in and focus on the vibration of love. My alignment to awareness, presence, and frequency guides me to the fulfillment of my expanding being. Everything I went through was nothing compared to what love has taught me.

◇◇◇◇◇◇◇◇◇◇◇

Ten days after the Lourdes trip, I took a weekend workshop, some kind of energetic modality. I didn't exactly know what the workshop was about, but that bossy voice told me to sign up. On the first day of the workshop, I sat in the third row, warming my ass with my zafu meditation pillow. Zara sat next to me on my left. I had the strange feeling that I knew her, yet I didn't know from where. She didn't resemble anyone I knew. Trying to figure it out, I recalled when I lit a candle at Lourdes and what I prayed for. *Love.* After that, when I dreamed, there was a beautiful, tall, and lean woman with dark brown silky-straight hair with bangs and the face of an angel. After making an impression on my psyche, I'd fallen madly in love with her. Every fiber of my being told me that Zara was the woman in those dreams.

I wasn't able to get Zara off my mind. Each time I saw her and heard her British accent, a swarm of butterflies landed in my stomach and migrated toward my throbbing heart. It was so intense that I felt I had disintegrated into subatomic particles whenever I was next to her. I'd never experienced anything close to this. I mustered the courage necessary to tell her that I'd fallen madly in love with her over the months. When I told Zara, I died, falling prey to an indescribable ecstasy, which took courage. I needed it to surrender to love.

Surprisingly, Zara told me she felt the same.

"This is bigger than you and me," I admitted.

"Indeed it is. We somehow found each other after bursting from the same fractal 13.8 billion years ago, and here we are with faces and smiles!" Zara said.

Nearly six months later, Zara invited me to dinner. Following behind her when she walked onto the perfectly lit patio in Malibu Farm, I inconspicuously admired every square inch of her, from split ends to toes. Her dark, shoulder-length brown hair shimmered in the light. She wore a relaxed black leather jacket with the front unzipped. Zippers can be inviting. She wore leggings with a tattoo design under a short skirt. She was badass punk chic! I lost my appetite for sashimi and wanted to devour her instead.

13.

Dance Away, My Precious Child

N DEEP CONTEMPLATION, I SIPPED A MUG OF HOT water when the most random thought hit me like a brick. *I'm going home to dance as Baby Jesus!* There was a festival in my village, where we celebrate and honor the royal child Jesus through dance. It's a massive event of great significance in the Philippines, but somehow I managed to evade it growing up. I never attended one, nor had any desire to dance in it. It's not uncommon to dress as a biblical figure for the dance, but no one dances *as* Baby Jesus. That would be blasphemy—or would it? I called Sissy.

"I'm dancing at the festival," I announced excitedly.

"You don't say things like that unless you're really going to do it," she said indignantly.

"I know what I said. I'm coming home. Getting my flight right now."

I didn't tell Sissy that, inspired by my visit to Lourdes, I wanted to dance *as* the child Jesus and that it was an order directly from Baby Jesus. It would have freaked her out. I didn't know how I was supposed to accomplish that, but somehow I would. The problem was that the Baby Jesus was in total regal vestments. Where was I going to find all that shit in a poor village? It didn't matter; I wasn't supposed to figure it out. It was clear my steps were being ordered. There was a voice—a very commanding voice that I could not ignore, telling me what to do. It wasn't new; it was always there. My hearing just improved over time, and I was growing and progressing monumentally. I began feeling, hearing, seeing, thinking, and acting in ways that surprised me. Somehow without making complete sense, it felt right.

The day before I left the States for Manila, I went to a barbershop and got a haircut that was so drastic the barber was confused when I described the style to him.

"Mohawk?" the barber asked, handing me a mirror to check myself out.

"No. And I don't need to see it. I can feel it. It's intense," I assured him.

"Are you sure?" he asked again.

"I trust you."

When he was finished, I paid him and walked out the door.

The American barber had seen all kinds of hair but was shocked to see me with that type of hairstyle. Maybe that's why I didn't want to see it. Typically, I don't look at my hair. I just know it's there, doing its thing or not doing anything. Regardless, it amuses me to see other people's extreme reactions to it, as though it's their hair. How dare I do something like that.

◇◇◇◇◇◇◇◇◇◇

Heading for the village I grew up in on a motorcycle through a snaky dirt road laden with deep potholes and muddy areas was tricky. The motorcycle was one mode of transportation that I opted for on that trip. The village was about a half-hour ride from the main highway where all the motorcycle taxis parked, waiting to service the locals. I traveled light with a carry-on that could fit between the motorcycle driver's legs. The ride helped acclimate me to local mode, seeing the stretch of rice paddy fields, the different fruit trees along the way: mango, lots of coconuts, grapefruits, guavas, jackfruit, star apple. Ah! I could smell home. Passing by a few villages, the houses were sparse. The river running parallel to the road was a sign I had entered the village. I took a deep sigh and observed the similar architectural design, bamboo and straw, that many homes had. But I could see people were tired of constant renovations with that style, and concrete became more prevalent.

The motorcycle stopped in front of an unfinished concrete structure, larger than most. I got off and stood still in front of it.

"Is this my house?"

My sister stood behind me, reassuring, "This is the house."

It was only halfway rebuilt, but it already looked much better than the house I had grown up in. On the outside, it looked like it needed a lot of work, but inside, it felt a lot more like home. I had a craving for lato, my favorite seaweed. It's translucent green like small grapes and eaten fresh with salt, vinegar, and sliced ginger. I wanted to eat, drink, and bathe in coconut juice. In America, a small bottle costs a fortune.

Although I wanted to dance as the child Jesus, I still needed to pitch the idea of dancing at the festival to someone in charge of the programming, then make some type of regal-looking costume. I didn't know how the dance would go because it's tribal. Worst-case scenario, I would just wing it MC Hammer–style. I thought I could pull it off, although generally, people who dance in that festival rehearse three months before the performance. It's a serious event. I knew I should practice at least a few times so I didn't embarrass my family, especially since it seemed I was a bit of a celebrity to them. It wasn't anything I'd done—the status was automatically earned simply coming from America. But I still reminded myself, *Don't get used to it, girl. No one's going to be serving you breakfast, lunch, and dinner unless you go to a restaurant.*

About a city block away from Mama's house is the village church, and I attended a service. There weren't many people, so I sat in the front row. In his late thirties, leading the mass, the youngest priest kept looking at me during the sermon. He appeared distracted by my presence. If I were to transcribe his thoughts, they would read like this: *This person must be from seven mountains away from some strange tribe.*

He's right. I imagine myself like *The Last of the Mohicans*, sticking a shark tooth to dangle from my nose to make it official.

It was nice to see my older brother assist with mass. Afterward, the priest came down from the altar to join my brother who then introduced me to the priest—who still thought I was from some strange tribe.

"Father, this is my sister," my older brother said. The priest looked at me like he was about to faint before quickly yet discreetly turning around to recalibrate his brain. I let him have his moment, and he turned back to face me with a fresh slate on his face. He had heard I was coming home and looked forward to meeting me. It sounded weird to call him Father because he seemed a lot younger than me. He probably went into the seminary at the age of three. I was told that the priest had adopted my family as his own. When he realized who I was, I felt a warm kindred spirit with him.

Exiting the church, I came across a distant relative, a woman and her daughter about seven years old. After third cousins, everyone falls into the distant relative category in a village like ours. The woman flat out told me, "My daughter wanted to know if something was wrong with you with your hair like that?"

Bending down to level with the child, I said to the girl in a pace slower than normal so the mother could hear too, "There's nothing wrong with me. I got this haircut because I wanted to, and I will try a different hairstyle after this. Some I might like more than others, but it's always fun." The little girl soaked up every syllable that came out of my mouth. I wanted her to know she should not be afraid to be different, and it's good to be who you want, as that is who you are—it's a part of self-love.

That evening, there was a big dinner at my house. It's weird to say "my house" because I don't live there; Mama does, but she refuses to accept ownership. She insisted it was mine. Maybe I have an issue with owning things.

I was hiding in my mother's room. My room was on the second floor, only that was still in the works. We just finished the first floor, and it looked good and was quite livable. When dinner was ready, they called me. I didn't know who was coming to dinner until I sat down at one end, and the priest took a seat next to me. I barely recognized him without his vestments. He was wearing cargo shorts and a faded striped shirt.

"Well, hello, Father," I said. If I didn't have Baby Jesus swirling in my head, I would have entertained the thought of hooking him up with my girlfriend in the States. He started talking about yoga and meditation. And how they, the Catholic Church, had adopted the practice of Eastern meditation to balance the Western practice. I was impressed that he knew about yoga. I didn't expect him to strike up that conversation. Before I could ramble on about things, the voice told me to pitch him my Baby Jesus dance—he was in charge of the festival programming.

"So, Father," I began. "From Los Angeles, I came all the way here to dance. My dance is not a performance but an offering of gratitude. So, it is imperative that I dance solo as Baby Jesus, symbolizing the royal child in each one of us." I had to hit him with it before he could interrupt my pitch.

He looked at me with a quiet receptivity.

Without hesitation, he replied, "Then you must do it." I was shocked at how it landed. "I'll add you to the program as a surprise number," he concluded.

That was easy. *Oh shit*, I said to myself. *This is getting real.* No one had ever danced solo. They're ensembles consisting of thirty to forty dancers in a group. There were seven ensemble troupes from different villages competing for a prize. And I still had to decide what I would do for a costume.

That night, I started gluing gold glitter speckles on a pair of boots. But I didn't feel they were what I wanted for the occasion. At a loss, fear and uncertainty began to settle in. *This is not happening*, I thought.

The next day, my older brother's daughter came over. They lived directly across the street. My niece was headed to the city and asked if I needed anything.

"Yes, I need to buy some cloth to make my costume."

She said she knew someone who could make the costume for me. I went with her, and we hunted that fella down. When I called, I demanded gracefully that he and I should meet as soon as possible. He gave us his address in the city, and in no time, my niece and I were knocking on his door. When *she* answered, there stood a flamboyant, larger-than-life personality. *She* showed me an elaborate gown she was working on. And before she could ramble on, I interrupted her, "I need you to make me a Baby Jesus costume. And I need it done in two weeks." She knew exactly what I was talking about, but when she opened her mouth, I didn't like what came out.

"I'm working on a couple of these gowns," she said pointing them out. "I'm super busy. I'm sorry, I don't think . . . "

She tried to spit out the rest of it, but I had to cut her off again, slapping two hundred dollars in her hand. Locking eyes like a Jedi, I insisted, "Two weeks. You can do it. Thank you!"

She closed her fist without uttering another word as we walked out the door.

I had the next two weeks to learn the dance. I tried to get the local band and drummers together for the live accompaniment and find someone to teach me the steps and choreography. But for some reason, it seemed impossible to get everyone together in the same place at the same time. Besides, I didn't know who all those people were, so I managed with what I had. Even Sissy tried to show me the steps, but they didn't seem to fit or make sense.

"That will not do!" I said to her. "I'm dancing solo. Do you see the whole stage arena I have to cover to fill up the whole space? It's not going to be small steps. It has to be so much bigger than life and one hundred times larger than the audience!"

Given there was no rehearsal, that wasn't happening.

The day before the festival, my Baby Jesus costume arrived. From the shoes to the crown, everything fit perfectly. She didn't even take measurements. I looked as amazingly regal as the Baby Jesus could. The costume was magnificent, and I wasn't worried; the rest would figure itself out.

A big flood hit the village at three in the morning. Everyone in the village watched as the flood turned into an oceanic blanket. There was no evacuation plan. No one came to rescue anyone. Some of the houses were halfway submerged, and several random items floated away. As for Mama's house, the water level was about five inches below floor level. We had raised the foundation three feet, mainly to avoid flooding. By the looks of it, I should have raised it three meters. Oddly, everyone seemed to be in great spirits. It became nothing but an opportunity for everyone to be together, knowing we were all in the same boat.

Mama went into her prayer routine, and I went back to Mama's room, lit a candle, and meditated. I prayed that the flood came to pass before sunrise with everyone safe. Seemingly, my prayer was three times longer than Mama's, so she joined me. She also prayed for everyone to be safe. Then, of course, the part where she prayed for it to rain men was so robust that I should have been flooded with husbands if it were up to her. After the meditation, feeling quite warm, I thanked her for joining me and appreciated that Mama said she liked doing my meditation.

I turned to face her and said, "Mama, there are hundreds of right men out there. None of them are right for me. I'm going to be with a woman. She's beautiful inside and out. How do you feel about me being with a woman?"

Mama was taking it to heart. I could see her brain cranking. She took a moment to digest it, and I was confident she heard me—and understood. I had never had that kind of intimate heart-to-heart space with Mama, *ever.*

After a long pause, Mama spoke conscientiously. "I have several concerns. One, God created man and woman to procreate."

"Yeah, and? Did you know people used to think the earth was flat?" Okay, that didn't land. Try again, girl. Sigh. "Well, God created more than man and woman. He also created man and man, woman and woman, and all variations in between."

Again, she took it in. I appreciated that we were two people openly exchanging thoughts. I listened with utter respect, no judgment, addressing her concerns thoughtfully without expectation, and Mama did the same.

"What do Amelia and Asia think of this?"

Even when Mama visited for six months, she was never

around Amelia and Asia. She didn't know how we were with each other.

"It's something we don't have to discuss. They understand," I told her flatly.

I wanted to take that chance to share something vital to me. I didn't want to wait to give of myself. That way, I could live my life by giving what I had now, not what I didn't get back then.

"What if this woman wants children? You can't give her children," she said, shaking her head.

"Are you sure about that? Remember, an angel announced to Mary that she would be pregnant with a son, then comes Jesus. Jesus, for Christ's sake!"

So far, so good. *Bring it on*, I said to myself.

"What if she realizes she needs a husband, and you need a husband?"

"I don't want to be with anyone because I need them. And I don't want anyone to be with me for that same reason. I want to be with someone because we love each other. And because we love unconditionally, we bring the very best version of each other."

She was processing—thinking things through and thinking some more. Making sure she got all fronts covered and had exhausted all avenues of converting me otherwise. Then came the big moment. Her Majesty went to a verdict, and I was pretty humbled by the opportunity to have that discussion. When I looked up at Mama's face, it softened with graceful acceptance.

"You have made it on your own. I couldn't have done what you did. You've grown strong and beautiful."

I showed Mama a picture of me and Zara and said, "She awakens the true love that I am."

Mesmerized by the photo, Mama said, "When it comes to matters of the heart, who am I to tell you what you should do?

I have great respect and immense admiration for you and the choices you've made. I give you all my blessings."

Oh my God, I felt my heart being squeezed, and it hurt so good. We leaned in and hugged. It was the best and warmest hug of them all. Why? It felt like complete acceptance and love rolled into one.

"I love you, Mama."

"I love you too," she replied.

For the very first time, I felt my mother's *unconditional* love seeping into every vein to nourish my atriums and ventricles. I had finally discovered self-love, so I knew what love, real love, felt like.

◇◇◇◇◇◇◇◇◇◇◇

By 6:00 a.m. the flood had receded by about 90 percent. Someone had lost their cow, but other than that, no casualties. It was the day of the festival, and I was slipping into the regal Baby Jesus costume. Many different villagers came to witness and pay homage to Señor Santo Niño, what I called Baby Jesus. The stage was a roundabout with the audience on all sides. The panel of judges sat in the front on an elevated platform. Since my surprise number came after all the troupes, I was up with the judges and had a chance to witness the ensembles dance. In the middle of the first dance troupe, the rain started to pour heavily, but the dance continued with all unfazed by the heavy downpour. Despite the unfavorable weather, even the spectators continued watching.

I mumbled, "I will dance rain or shine, but I would prefer the rain stops and the sun shines. And I don't mind the mud. So please, God, it would be so much more fun to dance with the sun shining and my cape flowing in the air, even though I'm shaking uncontrollably at this moment."

Watching seven troupes dance their numbers wearing elaborate costumes and choreography made me extremely nervous.
Hardly containing my nerves, I shook like a wet, cold dog. Then,
just as the last troupe was about to exit the arena, my nervousness soared off the chart. The heavy rain came to an abrupt halt,
and the sun was shining. That's a good sign. Always look at the
bright side, especially in times of utter nervousness.

I thought, *What in the hell was I talking about dancing solo. That
was nothing more than a planned disaster. Girl, look what trouble
you got yourself into this time.* I didn't even know what the drum
accompaniment sounded like or how long I'd stand there with
everyone staring at me. Oh well, I was catching a flight the next
day—they'd never see me again. I had all of those unpleasant
thoughts ruminating on an imagined predicament, and it would
have caused my nervous system to go into breakdown mode, but
it was too late—the host announced the surprise number—*me*!

Backstage battling the nervousness, I was about to step into
the arena without knowing what to do with myself. I tried ne-
gotiating with the program manager backstage about letting me
dance with one of the groups so I could kind of blend in. He said
okay, probably because he saw how nervous I was, but I knew
that was too good to be true. Dancing as the Baby Jesus was a
solo deal, but there I was, resisting the eventful process—the
most anticipated dance. After all, no one had ever seen the royal
kid dance live. It's always the people dancing for the child Jesus.
It was too late to back out. As soon as the announcement of my
surprise number went out, the audience of local and surrounding
villagers began talking about my solo dance.

As I stepped onto the stage arena, my nervousness wore me
out. All of a sudden, with grace, all the resistance dissolved.
And I heard the voice say, "My sweet child, relax. I'm dancing
through you. All this is my idea. Even *you* are my idea. I don't

need rehearsal. Every moment, I give birth to an infinitude of love, life, beauty, and joy. You showed up. You've done your part. Let me do the rest. Enjoy the ride. I'll be with you always."

Not long ago, a farmer named Severino founded our village. Along with his two brothers and sister, they were the first settlers. Back then, that place was one thick, lush roadless jungle. They cultivated it into a farm. He was a very simple and uneducated man but not lacking intelligence. In his unusual way of farming, he always threw the seeds in the river. The ones that came back were the ones they picked for seedlings. Pretty much, he wore a loincloth. G-string. One day, a plague of infestation hit the village. By then, the population had grown, and Severino was puzzled about what was eating up all the vegetation and causing great famine. A child came into his dream declaring he would wipe out the infestation. The following morning, he was in the river again, and he found a rock formed like a child. He didn't pay much attention and threw it away. But every day he kept finding the same rock. Finally, he examined it. Its form was just like the child in his dream. Severino began to honor the child, making offerings and rituals. This child was the regal Baby Jesus. And because of my connection, and my journey, I felt quite fitting that I should make the offering. Unbeknownst to me, *Severino was my grandfather.*

The *granddaughter* is dancing, the villagers said.

The other thing about Severino is that he was a hard-core shaman, often traveling to other dimensions. He was probably more involved in these invisible realms of ventures than he ever was in the visible world. That was another reason I ran away from the village. It sounds crazy, but I didn't want to be his successor. I wasn't aware of his profound impact on me until then—when I was draped in that regal vestment as Baby Jesus. Truth be told, his legend haunted me on the subconscious level, undeniably shaping the course of my life's journey. I didn't see myself in a G-string riding the dragon. The creature conveniently goes invisible when it comes to the minimal day-to-day job.

"Grandpa," I whispered, "I'm sorry—but not really. I will have to be you in a Deja way. My infinite gratitude to the Universe and its grand designer. To the ceaseless flow of unconditional love—the essence of who I am. With an open heart, this dance is for you."

With these words, I found myself and every cell in my body standing as the regal Baby Jesus. And I still had no clue how to dance. But in that very moment I came to fully embrace that unknown just as I had on every part of my journey thus far. I stood solemnly, taking a moment to acknowledge the audience, bowing graciously on all fronts. The audience grew silent in acknowledgment of the regal child in center stage. Then the first drum beat reverberated, thrusting my body into a flying leap with my red sequins and gold royal cape spread like eagle wings. My heart beat fast in ecstatic rhythm, singing in love as I communed with the audience through the offering. My soul danced in blissful joy in the center stage of my open heart. Boundless. I felt a deep sense of oneness to all.

The entire dance lasted about five minutes. When I heard one singular, loud drumbeat prompting me to slow down, I dropped to my knees, bowing all the way, and kissed Mother Earth. At that moment of realization, I understood that I had arrived at the abode of joyful being within. All along, the love I had tirelessly pursued to the farthest reaches of the world was now—or rather, had perpetually been—gracefully dancing with me, devotedly existing for me, and radiantly flowing through every fiber of my being.

ACKNOWLEDGMENTS

I am deeply grateful to my dear family and friends, whose love and support have mirrored my growth and healing. I am also thankful for everyone and everything who conspired for my soul's awakening and to the Divine for its pervading, inescapable presence.

A heartfelt thank you to my editors, Mensah Demary and Dan López, and the incredible team at Catapult and Counterpoint, for holding a supportive space that nurtured my authentic voice throughout the intense process of self-excavation.

DEJA VU PREM is a filmmaker originally
from the Philippines.